BHAGVAD GEETA GYAN

BHAGVAD GEETA GYAN

Manmohan Sharma

Publications

KALPAZ PUBLICATIONS

Delhi - 110052

Bhagvad Geeta Gyan

ISBN : 81-7835-409-5

Published in 2007 in India by
Kalpaz Publications
C-30, Satyawati Nagar, Delhi - 110052
Phone : 9212729499
e-mail : kalpaz@hotmail.com

Laser Typesetting at : Vinayak Printers, Delhi
Printed at : Salasar Imaging System, Delhi

The Utmost Message of The Bhagvad Geeta Gyan Self Assessment

- *Whatever has happened, that has happened for Goodness.*
- *Whatever is happening now that is happening for goodness indeed.*
- *Whatever will it happen, that shall be for goodness too.*
- *What have we lost, for that we are sad?*
- *What did we bring with us, which are we lost?*
- *What did we create, which has ruined?*
- *We didn't bring any thing, when we came to this world.*
- *Whatever we have, that was already in this world.*
- *Whatever we give, that we only return to this world.*
- *We came at our own, thus we shall return at our own too.*
- *Whatever belongs to us today, that was some one else before.*
- *And the same remain will be with someone else in future.*
- *Change is the ultimate function of Thee–Divine.*
- *Thus what we are and for what we are too?*
- *We are just the function of Thee–Divine.*
- *Thus our every function shall be the same of Thee–Divine.*

Contents

Preface

After years of intense searching for the ultimate ever existing peace of mind in my current life-cycle I was automatically blessed with the utmosd realized spiritual theme of **The Almighty** functions within every living beings which further encouraged me to translate the words of speech, pronounced by a great philosopher of the time **Bhagwan: Shree Krishan Ji** to his chum, a prince with a great moral values including with the utmost qualities of a successful soldier, **Prince: Aurjun**, quoted innermost secrets of the **Bhagvad Geeta Gyan** compiled by a great **Saint: Shree Ved Vias**. The **philosophy** confirms every reader or even as a listener that how to properly apply the **Bhagvad Geeta Gyan** in all times, places and under the circumstance, so one could constantly live in an exalted spiritually enlightened state of consciousness. The knowledge of the Universe clearly alleviates the suffering that is so much running rampant in today's world.

The Bhagvad Geeta-Gyan, the knowledge of the Universe has been composed, into the **English** language to reinforce the common understanding within every living beings, through out the entire Universe. It is designed for everyone, including the beginners who have just achieved a variety of some Spiritual knowledge through their day to day life experience and are now equally interested to extend and realize their **utmost, The Almighty** functions, based upon the fundamental principles of the eternal aliments of **Thy Glory**.

The Bhagvad Geeta Gyan, confirms and guides that it is the only ingenuity of expedient, through whihc any one can practice to understand the reality that, ultimately there is the only one **Supreme**, the creator of all living beings. Thus all the creations come from and the same return to **Thy Glory**.

The ones' who adopt and follow the principles of **Thy-Glory** in life, they are the ones' who live forever but the ones' who later begin to misuse those powers, create an unpleasant and unstable society, in which the lives of all the people become unbearable. Then the **Supreme**, presents **Thyself** into those living beings, the ones' who are just about to enter into the heaven and then creates a balance of power between good and evil by counteracting and gradually diffusing the evil force that exists to maintain peace and happiness on the earth.

The knowledge of the **Bhagvad Geeta Gyan** is distilled for the reader the finest essence of what I have imbibed from my long life experience as a practitioner of this wonderful science of self-realization. I am sure that you will find this task to be interesting and most helpful for your spiritual advancement.

With the blessing of **Thy-Glory ...**

Dr. Manmohan Sharma (UK)

Composer, designer and translator into the English language.

August, 1985

1

Observing the Armies on the Battlefield of Kurukshetra

The King Dhritarashtr Asked his Chief Secretary, Shree Sanjay;

1. Please tell me, what is going on between my sons and my brother Pandu's sons who are now assembled at the battlefield to perform their duties.

Shree Sanjay Said:

2. On seeing the Pandu's army drawn up in battle array, prince: Duryodhan approached Dron Acharya, the preceptor, and addressed him thus:

3. Behold, dear preceptor, this mighty army of Pandu – family, set in array by the son of, King Drupad, thy wise disciple.

4. Here are brave bowmen, peers of Bhim and Arjun in fighting: Yuyudhan and Virata, and the 'Maharathi' Drupada.

5. Dhrishtaketu, Chekitana, valorous Kashiraja, Purujit the Kuntibhoja, and Shaibya, chief among men;

6. Valiant Yudhamanyu, valorous Uttamaujas, Subhadra's son, and the sons of Draupadi each one of them a 'Maharathi'.

7. Acquaint Thyself now, the best of Brahman, with the distinguished among us.

I mention for Thy information, the names of the captains of my army. I mention for Thy information, the names of the captains of my army. I mention for Thy information, the names of the captains of my army.

8. Thy noble self, Bhishm, Karn, and Kripa Achrya, victorious in battle, Ashvatthama, Vikarna, also Somadatta's son;

9. There are many another hero's, known for their skills in wielding diverse weapons, pledged to lay down their lives for my sake, and all adepts in war.

10. This our force, commanded by Bhishm Pitama, is all too inadequate; while theirs, commanded by Bhim, is quite adequate.

11. Therefore, let each of you, holding your appointed places, at every entrance, guard only Bhishm Pitama.

12. At this, the heroic grandsire, the grand old man of the Kurus, gave a loud lion's roar and blew his conch to hearten Duryodhan.

13. There upon, conches, drums, cymbals and trumpets were sounded all at once.

    Terrific was the noise.

14. Then Madhav and Pandav, standing in their great chariot yoked with white steeds, blew their Divine conches.

15. Hrishikesha blew the Panchajanya and Dhananjaya the Devadatta; while the wolf – bellied Bhim of dread deeds sounded his great conch Paundra.

16. King Yudhishthir, Kunti's son, blew the Anantavijaya, and Nakul nd Sahdev their conches, Sughosha and Manipushpaka.

17. And Kashiraj, the great bowman, Shikhandi the 'Maharatha', Dhrishtadyumna, Virata and Satyaki, the unconquerable.

18. Drupad, Draupadi's sons, the strong – armed son of Subhadra, all these, dear King, blew each his own conch.

19. That terrifying tumult, causing earth and heaven to resound, rent the hearts of king Dhritarashtr's sons.

20. Then, dear King, the ape – bannered Pandav, seeing king Dhritarashtr's sons, arrayed and flight of arrows about to begin, took up his bow, and spoke thus to Hrishikesh: "Set my chariot between the two armies, dear : Keshav!"

22. That I may behold them drawn up, on battle intent, and know whom I have to engage in this fearful combat.

23. And that I may survey the fighters assembled here anxious to fulfil in battle perverse prince: Duryodhan's desire.

Sanjay Said:

24-25. Thus addressed by Gudakesh, dear King, Hrishikesh set the unique chariot between the two armies in front of Bhishm, Dron – Achria and all the kings and said: Behold, dear Parth, the Kurus assembled yonder.

26-27. Then did Parth see, standing there, sires, grandsires, preceptors, uncles, see, brothers, sons, Grandsons, comrades, fathers brothers, fathers - in - law and friends in both armies.

Beholding all these kinsmen ranged before him, Kauntey was overcome with great compassion and spoke thus in anguish:

Arjun Said:

28-29. As I look upon these kinsmen, dear Krishn, assembled here eager to fight, my, limbs fail, my mouth is parched, a tremor shakes my frame and my hair stands on end.

30. Gandiv slips from my hand, my skin is on fire, I cannot keep my feet, and my mind reels.

31. I have unhappy forebodings, dear Keshav; and I see no good in slaying kinsmen in; battle.

32. I seek not victory, nor sovereign power, nor earthly joys. What good are sovereign power, worldly pleasures and even life to us, dear Govind?

33. Those for whom we would desire sovereign power, earthly joys and delights are here arrayed in battle, having renounced life and wealth.

34. Preceptors, sires, grandsires, sons and even grandsons, uncles, fathers - in - law, brothers - in - law, and other kinsmen.

35. These I would not kill, dear Madhusudan, even though they slay me, not even for, kingship of the three worlds, much less for an earthly kingdom.

36. What pleasure can there be in slaying these sons of Dhritarashtr, dea Janardana? Sin only can be our lot, if we slay these, usurpers though they be.

37. It does not therefore behove us to kill our kinsmen, these sons of king Dhritarashtr.

How may we be happy, dear Madhav, in killing our own kin?

38. Even though these, their wits warped by greed, see not the guilt that lies in destroying the family, nor the sin of treachery to comrades.

39. How can we, dear Janardan, help recoiling from this sin, seeing clearly as we do the, guilt that lies in such destruction?

40. With the destruction of the family perish the eternal family virtues, and with the perishing of these virtues unrighteousness seizes the whole family.

41. When unrighteousness prevails, dear Krishn, the women of the family become, corrupt, and their corruption, dear Varsh, causes a confusion of Varn (family).

42. This confusion verily drags the family – slayer, as well as the family, to hell, and for want of obsequies offerings and rites their departed sires fall from blessedness.

43. By the sins of these family – slayers resulting in confusion of varn (Description), the eternal tribal and family virtues are brought to naught.

44. For we have had it handed down to us, dear Janardan, that the men whose family, virtues have been ruined are doomed to dwell in hell.

45. Alas! What a heinous sin we are about to commit, in that, from greed of the joy of sovereign power, we are prepared to slay our kith and kin!

46. Happier far would it be for me if king Dhritarashtr's sons, weapons in hand, should strike me down on the battlefield, unresisting and unarmed.

Sanjaya Said:

47. Thus spoke Arjun on the field of battle, and dropping his bow 'Gandiv' and arrows sank down on his seat in the chariot, overwhelmed with anguish.

2

Summarized the Contents of the Bhagvad Geeta Gyan

Sanjay Said:

1. To Arjun, thus overcome with compassion, sorrowing, and his eyes obscured by flowing tears, dear Madhusudan Bhagwan: Shree Krishan) speaks these words:

Bhagwan: Shree Krishan Said:

2. How is it that at this perilous moment this delusion, unworthy of the noble, leading neither to heaven nor to the Divine,, has overtaken Thee?

3. Yield not to unmanliness, dear Parth; it does not become thee. Shake off this miserable faint heartedness and arise, dear Parantap (a great personality)!

Arjun Said:

4. How shall I, with arrows, engage Bhishm and Dron in battle, dear Madhusudan, they who are worthy of reverence, dear Arisudan?

5. It were better far to live on alms of this world than to slay these venerable elders. Having slain them I should but have blood stained enjoyments.

6. Nor do we know which is better for us, that we conquer them or that they conquer us, for here stand before us Dhritarashtr's sons having killed whom we should have no desire to live.

7. My being is paralysed by faint heartedness; my mind discerns not duty; hence I ask thee; tell me, I pray thee, in no uncertain language, wherein lies my good. I am Thy disciple; please guide me, I see refuge in Thee.

8. For I see nothing that can dispel the anguish that shrivels up my senses even if I should win on earth uncontested sovereignty over a thriving kingdom or Thy Glory over the Supreme.

Sanjay Said:

9. Thus spoke Parantap to Hrishikesh Govind, and with the words 'I will not fight' and became speechless.

10. To him thus stricken with anguish, dear Bharat (The symbol of independence)! between the two armies, Hrishikesh, as though mocking, addressed these words:

Bhagwan: Shree Krishan Said:

11. Thou mournest for them whom thou should not mourn and utters vain words of wisdom. The wise mourn neither for the living nor for the dead.

12. For never was I not, nor thou, nor these kings; nor will any of us cease to be hereafter.

13. As the embodied one has, in the present body, infancy, youth and age, even so does he receive another body. The wise man is not deceived therein.

14. Dear Kaunteya! contacts of the senses with their objects bring cold and heat, pleasure and pain; they

come and go and are transient. Endure them, dear Bharat.

15. Dear noblest of men, the wise man who is not disturbed by these, who is unmoved by pleasure and pain, he is fitted for immortality.

16. What is non being is never known to have been, and what is being is never known not to have been. of both these the secret has been seen by the seers of the Truth.

17. Just know that to be imperishable whereby all this is pervaded. No one can destroy that immutable being.

18. These bodies of the embodied one who is eternal, imperishable and immeasurable are finite. Fight, therefore, dear Bharat.

19. The One, who thinks of This Aatama as slayer and the One, who believes This to be slain, are both ignorant. This neither slays nor is ever slain.

20. The Aatma is never born nor ever dies, nor having been will ever not be any more; unborn, eternal, everlasting, ancient, This is not slain when the body is slain.

21. The ones who knows this, dear Parth, to be imperishable, eternal, unborn, and immutable whom and how can that person slay or cause to be slain?

22. As we all the human beings off worn out clothes and takes others that are new, even so the embodied one casts off worn out bodies and passes on to others new.

23. This no weapons wound, This no fire burns, This no waters wet, This no wind doth dry.

24. Beyond all cutting, burning, wetting and drying is this eternal, all pervading, stable, immovable, everlasting.

25. Perceivable neither by the senses nor by the mind, This is called unchangeable; therefore knowing This as such thou should not grieve.

26. And if thou deems this to be always coming to birth and always dying, even then, dear Maha Bahu, thou should not grieve.

27. For certain is the death of the born, and certain is the birth of the dead; therefore what is unavoidable thou should not regret.

28. The state of all beings before birth is un-manifest; their middle state manifest; their state after death is again un - manifest. What occasion is there for lament, dear Bharat?

29. One looks upon This as a marvel; another speaks of this as such; another hears thereof as a marvel; yet having heard this none truly knows this.

30. This embodied one in the body of every being is ever beyond all harm, dear Bharat; thou should not, therefore, grieve for any one.

31. Again, seeing own duty thou should not shrink from it; for there is no higher good for a Kshatriy than a righteous war.

32. Such a fight, coming unsought, as a gateway to heaven thrown open, falls only to the lot of happy Kshatriy, dear Parth.

33. But if thou wilt not fight this righteous fight, then failing in thy duty and losing honour thou wilt incur sin.

34. The world will for ever recount the story of thy disgrace; and for a person of honour disgrace is worse than death.

35. The Maha Rathi will think that fear made thee retire from battle; and thou wilt fall in the esteem of those very ones who have held thee high.

36. Enemies will deride thy prowess and speak many unspeakable words about thee. What can be more painful than that?

37. Slain, thou shall gain heaven; victorious, thou shall inherit the earth: therefore arise, dear Kaunteya, determined to fight.

38. Hold alike pleasure and pain, gain and loss, victory and defeat, and gird up Thy loins for the fight; so doing thou shall not incur sin.

39. Thus have I set before thee the attitude of Knowledge; hear now the attitude of action; resorting to this attitude thou shall cast off the bondage of action.

40. Here no effort undertaken is lost, no disaster befalls. Even a little of this righteous course delivers one from great fear.

41. The attitude, in this matter, springing, as it does, from fixed resolve is but one, dear Kuru Nandan; but for those who have no fixed resolve the attitudes are many branched and unending.

42-44. The ignorant, revelling in the letter of the Ved (The knowledge of the universe), declare that there is naught else; carnally minded, holding Heaven to be their goal, they utter swelling words which promise birth as the fruit of action and which dwell on the many and varied rites to be performed for the sake of pleasure and power; intent, as they are, on pleasure and power their swelling words rob them of their wits, and they have no settled attitude which can be cantered on the supreme goal.

45. The Ved have as their domain the three Gun; eschew them, dear Arjun. Free Thyself from the pairs of opposites, abide in eternal truth, scorn to gain or guard anything, remain the Supreme of Aatma (Thy soul).

46. To the extent that a well is of use when there is a flood of water on all sides, to the same extent are all the Ved of use to an enlightened Brahm (Universe).

47. Action alone is thy province, never the fruits thereof; let not thy motive be the fruit of action, nor should thou desire to avoid action.

48. Act thou, dear Dhananjaya, without attachment, steadfast in Yog (Abilty), even minded in success and failure. Even mindedness is Yog.

49. For action, dear Dhananjaya, is far inferior to unattached action; seek refuge in the attitude of detached action. Pitiable are those who make fruit their motive.

50. Here in this world a person gifted with that attitude of detachment escapes the fruit of both good and evil deeds. Gird thyself up for Yog, therefore. Yog is skill in action.

51. For sages, gifted with the attitude of detachment, who renounce the fruit of action, are released from the bondage of birth and attain to the state which is free from all ills.

52. When thy understanding will have passed through the slough of delusion, then wilt thou be indifferent alike to what thou hast heard and wilt hear.

53. When thy understanding, distracted by much hearing, will rest steadfast and unmoved in concentration, then wilt thou attain Yog.

Arjun Said:

54. What, dear Keshav, is the mark of the man whose understanding is secure, whose mind is fixed in concentration? How does that One talk? How sit? How move.

Bhagwan: Shree Krishan Said:

55. When a person puts away, dear Parth, all the cravings that arise in the mind and finds comfort for own self only from Aatma, then is called the person of a secure understanding.

56. Whose mind is untroubled in sorrows or for joys, who is free from passion, fear and wrath, is called the ascetic of secure understanding.

57. Who owns attachment nowhere, who feels neither joy nor resentment whether good or bad comes own way that person's understanding is secure.

58. And when, like the tortoise drawing in its limbs from every side, this man draws in the One's senses from their objects, that One's understanding is secure.

59-60. When a person starves own senses, the objects of those senses disappear from the mind, but not the yearning for them; the yearning too departs when that One beholds the Supreme. For, in spite of the wise person's endeavour, dear Parath, the unruly senses distract his mind perforce.

61. Holding all these in check, the Yogi (Able) should sit intent on me; for one whose senses are under control is secure of understanding.

62. In a person brooding on objects of the senses, attachment to them springs up; attachment begets craving and craving begets wrath.

63. Wrath breeds stupefaction, stupefaction leads to loss

of memory, loss of memory ruins the reason, and the ruin of reason spells utter destruction.

64. But the disciplined soul, moving among sense objects with the senses weaned from likes and dislikes and brought under the control of Aatma, attains peace of mind.

65. Peace of mind means the end to all ills, for the understanding of that One's whose mind is at peace stands secure.

66. The undisciplined person has neither understanding nor devotion; for own who has no devotion there is no peace, and for own who has no peace whence happiness?

67. For when his mind runs after any of the roaming senses, it sweeps away his understanding, as the wind a vessel upon the waters.

68. Therefore, dear Maha Bahu, one, whose senses are reined in on all sides from their objects, is the person of secure understanding.

69. When it is night for all other beings, the disciplined soul is awake; when all other beings are awake, it is night for the seeing ascetic.

70. One in whom all longings subside, even as the waters subside in the ocean which, though ever being filled by them, never overflows that person finds peace; not one who cherishes longing.

71. The person who sheds all longing and moves without concern, free from the sense of 'Mine' that one attains peace.

72. This is the state, dear Parth, of the one who rests in Brahm; having attained to it that one is not deluded. One who abides in this state even at the hour of death passes into oneness with Brahm.

3

Karm Yog (The Eternal Functions of a Personal Ability)

Arjun Said:

1. If, dear Janardan, thou hold that the attitude of detachment is superior to action, then why, dear Keshav, dost thou urge me to dreadful action?

2. Thou dost seem to confuse my understanding with perplexing speech; tell me, therefore, in no uncertain voice, that alone whereby I may attain salvation.

Bhagwan: Shree Krishan Said:

3. I have spoken, before, dear sinless one, of two attitudes in this world the Sankshay 'Doubt, that of Gyan Yog and the Yogi', that of karm Yog.

4. Never does a person enjoy freedom from action by not undertaking action, nor does that One attain that freedom by mere renunciation of action.

5. For none ever remains inactive even for a moment; for all are compelled to action by the Gun (Qualities) inherent in prakriti (The fact in nature).

6. The One, who curbs the organs of action but allows the mind to dwell on the sense objects, such a one, wholly deluded, is called a hypocrite.

7. But the One, dear Arjun, who keeping all the senses under control of the mind, engages the organs in Karm Yog, without attachment that One's excels.

8. Do thou thy allotted task; for action is superior to inaction; with inaction even life's normal course is not possible.

9. This world of person suffers bondage from all action save that which is done for the sake of sacrifice; to this end, dear Kaunteya, perform action without attachment.

10. In the beginning, the creator created human beings together with selfless service (Serv Gyan, sacrifice) and said: By serving each other you shall prosper and the sacrificial service shall full fill all your desires.

11. With this may you cherish the gods and may the gods cherish you; thus cherishing one another may you attain the highest good.

12. Cherished with sacrifice, the Supreme will bestow on you the desired boons. One, who enjoys the gifts without rendering aught unto them is verily a thief.

13. The righteous person who eat the residue of the sacrifice are freed from all sin, but the wicked who cook for themselves eat sin.

14. From food springs all life, from rain is born food; from sacrifice comes rain and sacrifice is the result of action.

15. Know that action springs from Brahm and Brahm from the Imperishable; hence the all pervading Brahm is ever firm founded on sacrifice.

16. The one, who does not follow the wheel thus set in motion here below, that One, living in sin, sating on own senses, lives, dear Parath, in vain.

17. But the person who revels in Aatma, who is content in Aatma and who is satisfied only with Aatma, for that One no action exists.

18. The One has no interest whatever in anything done, nor in anything not done, nor has One's need to rely on anything for personal ends.

19. Therefore, do thou ever perform without attachment the work that thou must do, for performing action without attachment that One attains the Supreme.

20. For through action alone Gyan and others achieved perfection; even with a view to the guidance of human thou must act.

21. Whatever the best person does, is also done by other Ones, what example that One sets, the world follows.

22. For me, dear Parth, there is naught to do in the full Three Tenses (all ages) so is called this world, nothing worth gaining that I have not gained; yet I am ever in action.

23. Indeed, for were I not, un-slumbering, ever to remain in action, dear Parth, Ones would follow my example in every way.

24. If I were not to perform my function, this world (Creation) would be ruined; I should be the same cause of chaos and of the end of all living beings.

25. Just as, with attachment, the unenlightened perform all actions, dear Bharat, even so, but unattached, should the enlightened One act, with a desire for the welfare of humanity.

26. The enlightened may not confuse the mind of the unenlightened, who are attached to action; rather must he perform all actions unattached, and thus encourage them to do likewise.

27. All action is entirely done by the Gun (Qualities) of prakriti (The Nature). Ones, deluded by the senses, I am the doer'.

28. But One, dear Maha Bahu, who understands the truth of the various Gun and their various activities, knows that it is the Gun that operate on the Gun; One does not claim to be the doer.

29. Deluded by the Gun of prakriti, Ones become attached to the activities of the Gun; One who knows the truth of things should not unhinge the slow witted who have not the knowledge.

30. Cast all thy acts on me, with thy mind fixed on the indwelling Aatma, and without any thought of fruit, or sense of 'mine' shake off thy fever and fight!

31. Those who always act according to the rules I have here laid down, in faith and without cavilling, they too are released from the bondage of their actions.

32. But those who cavil at the rules and refuse to conform to it are fools, dead to all knowledge; know that they are lost.

33. Even One of knowledge acts according to Own nature; all creatures follow their nature; what then will constraint avail?

34. Each sense has its settled likes and dislikes towards its objects; that One should not come under the sway of these, for they are Ones best.

35. Better One's own duty, bereft of merit, than another's well performed; better is death in the discharge of one's duty; another's duty is fraught with danger.

Arjun Said:

36. Then what impels One to sin, dear Kashiv, even against that One's will, as though by force compelled?

Bhagwan: Shree Krishan Said:

37. It is Lust, it is Wrath, born of the Rajo Gun. It is the arch devourer, the arch sinner. Know this to be One's enemy here.

38. As fire is obscured by smoke, a mirror by dirt, and the embryo by the amnion, so is knowledge obscured by this.

39. Knowledge is obscured, dear Kaunteya, by this eternal enemy of the wise One, in the form of Lust, the insatiable fire.

40. The senses, the mind and the reason are said to be its great seat; by means of these it obscures knowledge and stupefies One.

41. Therefore, dear Bharat Shrasht, bridle thou first the senses and then rid Thyself of this sinner, the destroyer of knowledge and discrimination.

42. Subtle, they say, are the senses; subtler than the senses is the mind; subtler than the mind is the reason; but subtler even than the reason is that One's.

43. Thus realizing the functions of Thy Glory to be subtler than the reason, and controlling the self by the Aatma, destroy, dear Maha Bahu, this enemy, Lust, so hard to overcome.

4

The Knowledge of Meditation

Bhagwan: Shri Krishan Said:

1. I expounded this imperishable Yog to Vivasvat; Vivasvat communicated it through the Ved (System), and further to Iksh Vaku, the One, who first practised in the beginning.

2. Thus handed down in succession, the Royal sages learnt it; with long lapse of time it dwindled away in this world, dear Parantap.

3. The same ancient Yog, I have expounded to the today; for thou art my devotee and my chum this is the Supreme mystery.

Arjun Said:

4. Later was Thy birth, Shree Krishan, earlier that of Vivacious. How then am I to understand that Thou did expound it in the beginning?

Bhagwan: Shri Krishan Said:

5. Yes, many births have we passed through, dear Arjun, both thou and I know them all, thou know them not, dear Parantap.

7. For whenever right declines and wrong prevails, then dear Bharat, I take birth.

8. To save the righteous, to destroy the wicked, and to re-establish right I am born from age to age. (All periods)

9. The Ones, who know the secret of this my divine birth and action is not born again, after leaving the body; only those Ones return to me, dear Arjun.

9. The One, who knows the secret of this my Divine birth and action is not born again, after leaving the body; only that One comes to me, dear Arjun.

10. Freed from passion, fear and wrath, filled full with me, relying on me, and refined by the fiery ordeal of knowledge, many have become one with me.

11. In whatever way Ones resort to me, even so do I render to them. In every way, dear Parth, the One, who follows that path is mine.

12. The Ones, who desire their actions to bear fruit worship the Dev (Saints) here; for in this world of Ones, the fruit of action is quickly obtainable.

13. The order of the four Varn (Creative forms) was created by me according to the different Gun with karm (Qualities in functions) of each yet know that though, therefore, author thereof, being changeless I am not the author.

14. Actions do not affect me, nor am I concerned with the fruits (Result) thereof. The Ones, who recognizes me as such is not bound by actions.

15. Knowing this did Ones of old, desirous of freedom, perform action; do thou, then, just as they did, the Ones of old in days gone by.

16. What is action? What is inaction? Here even the wise are perplexed. I will then expound to thee that action knowing which thou shall be saved from evil.

17. For it is meet to know the meaning of action, of forbidden action, as also inaction.

Impenetrable is the secret of action.

18. The Ones, who see action in action and action in inaction, that One is enlightened among Ones, that One is Yogi, (Intelligent) who has done all Ones need to do.

19. The One, whose every undertaking is free from desire and selfish purpose, and that One who has burnt all personal actions in the fire of knowledge, such an one the wise call a Pandit or Perm Aatama.

20. The One who has renounced attachment to the fruit of action, who is ever content, and free from all dependence, that One, though immersed in action, yet acts not.

21. Expecting naught, holding his mind and body in check, putting away every possession, and going through action only in the body he incurs no stain.

22. Content with whatever chance may bring, rid of the pairs of opposites, free from ill will, even minded in success and failure, that One is not bound though One's acts.

23. Of the free Aatma (Soul) who has shred all attachment, whose mind is firmly grounded in knowledge, who acts only for sacrifice, all karm is extinguished.

24. The offering of sacrifice is Brahm; the oblation is Brahm; it is offered by Brahm in the fire that is Brahm; thus that One whose mind is fixed on acts dedicated to Brahm must needs pass on to Brahm.

25. Some Yogi perform sacrifice in the form of worship of the Dev, others offer sacrifice of sacrifice itself in the fire that is Brahm.

26. Some Ones offer as sacrifice the sense of hearing, the other senses in the fires of restraint; others sacrifice sound, while the other objects of sense in the fires of the senses.

27. The others again sacrifice all the activities of their senses and of the vital energy in the Yog fire of self-control kindled by knowledge.

28. Some sacrifice with material gifts; with austerities; with Yog; some with the acquiring and some with the imparting of knowledge. All these are sacrifices of stern vows and serious endeavour.

29. Others absorbed in the exercise of the control of the vital energy sacrifice the outward in the inward and the inward in the outward, or check the flow of both the inward and the outward vital airs.

30. Yet others, abstemious in food, sacrifice one form of vital energy in another. All these know what sacrifice is and purge themselves of all impurities by sacrifice.

31. Those who perform selfless service obtain the nectar (Amrit) of Self-knowledge as a result of their sacrifice and attain the Supreme Being. Dear Arjun, if this world is not a happy place for the non-sacrificing, how can the other world would be?

32. Even so various sacrifices have been described in the Ved; know them all to proceed from action; knowing this thou shall be released.

33. Dear Parantap, the knowledge of sacrifice is better, than material sacrifice, for all action which does not bind finds its consummation in knowledge.

34. Acquire this transcendental knowledge with a self-realization through humble reverence by sin-cere inquiry. Only those empowered Ones, can create the learning environment for others.

35. When thou hast gained this knowledge, dear Parth, thou shall not again fall into such error by virtue of it thou shall see all beings without exception in thyself and thus in me.

36. Even though thou be the most sinful of sinners, thou shall cross the ocean of sin by the boat of knowledge.

37. As a blazing fire turns its fuel to ashes, dear Arjun, even so the fire of knowledge turns all actions to ashes.

38. There is nothing in this world so purifying as knowledge. The Ones, who are perfected by Yog (Exercise) find it in own self in the fullness of time.

39. It is the person of faith, who gains such a knowledge that who is intent on it and who has build the supremacy over own senses; only that One comes ere long to the supreme peace.

40. The irrational, the faithless One, and the disbeliever perish. There is neither this world nor the world beyond nor happiness for a disbeliever.

41. The One, who has renounced all action by means of Yog, who has severed all doubt by the means of knowledge self-possessed, no actions bind! Dear Dhananjay.

42. Therefore, with the sword of Self-realization sever thou this doubt, bred of ignorance, which has crept into thy heart! Betake thyself to Yog and arise, dear Bharat!

5

Karm-Yog-Action in Consciousness

Arjun Said:

1. Thou loudest renunciation of actions, dear Shree Krishn, whilst at the same time thou loudest performance of action; tell me for a certainty which is the better aid?

Bhagwan: Shree Krishan:

2. Renunciation and performance of action both lead to salvation, but of the two, Karm-Yog is preferably better than Sannyas (renunciation).

3. A person should be considered a devotee to renunciation and who has neither attachment nor aversion for anything. One is easily liberated from Karm-Yog bondage by becoming free from attachment and aversion.

4. It is the ignorant who speak of Sankhaya and Yog as different, not so those who have knowledge. One, who is rightly established even in one wins to the fruit of both.

5. Whatever goal a renouncing reaches, a Karm-Yogi also reaches. Therefore, The One, who sees the path of renunciation and thc path of unselfish work as the same really sees.

6. But renunciation, dear Maha-Bahu, is hard to attain except by Yog-Karm; the ascetic equipped with Yog attains Brahm ere long.

7. A Karm-Yogi, whose mind is pure, whose mind and senses are under control, and who sees one and the same Spirit in all beings, is not bound by Karm though engaged in work.

8. The Yogi who has seen the Truth knows that it is not One, who acts whilst seeing, hearing, touching, smelling, eating, walking, sleeping, or breathing etc.

9. Talking, letting go, holding fast, opening or closing the eyes, in the conviction that is the senses that are moving in their respective spheres.

10. The One, who dedicates own actions to Brahm and performs them without attachment is not smeared by sin, as the lotus-leaf by water.

11. Only with the body, mind and intellect and also with the senses, do the Yogi perform action without attachment for the sake of self-purification.

12. A Yog-person obtains everlasting peace by abandoning the fruit of action; the One ignorant of Yog (Ability), selfishly attached to fruit, remains bound.

13. Renouncing with the mind all actions, the dweller in the body, who is in-charge of own-self, rests happily in own boy of nine passages, neither doing nor getting anything done.

14. Thy-Glory creates neither agency nor action for the world; neither does One connect action with its fruit. It is The Divine that is at function.

15. Thy-Glory does not take upon own-self anyone's vice

or virtue; it is ignorance that veils knowledge and deludes all creatures.

16. But to them whose ignorance is destroyed by the knowledge of Aatma, this their knowledge, like the sun, reveals the Supreme.

17. Those whose intellect is suffused with that, whose self has become one with that, who abide in that, and whose end and aim is that, wipe out their sins with knowledge, and go whence there is no return.

18. The One of Self-realization look with an equal eyes on a Brahm possessed of learning and humility, a cow, an elephant, a dog and even a dog-eater.

19. In this very body they have conquered the round of birth and death, whose mind is anchored in sameness; for perfect Brahm is same to all, therefore in Brahm they rest.

20. The One whose understanding is secure, who is undeluded, who knows Brahm and who rests in Brahm, will neither be glad to get what is pleasant, nor sad to get what is unpleasant.

21. The One, who has detached own-self from contacts without, finds bliss in Aatma having achieved union with Brahm only that One enjoys eternal bliss.

22. For the joys derived from sense-contacts are nothing but mines of misery; they have beginning and end, dear Kaunteya; the wise person does not revel therein.

23. The One, who is able even here on earth, ere One is released from the body, to hold out against the flood-tide of lust or wrath, that One is a Yogi (able), One, who is happy.

24. The One, who finds happiness only within, rest only

within, light only within, that Yogi, having become one with nature, attains to just oneness with Brahm.

25. They win oneness with Brahm, the seers whose sins are wiped out, whose doubts are resolved, who have supremacy over own-selves, and who are engrossed in the welfare of all beings.

26. Rid of lust and wrath, control of themselves, the ascetics who have realized Aatma find oneness with Brahm everywhere around them.

27-28. That ascetic is ever free who, having shut out the outward sense-contacts, sits with own gaze fixed between the brows, outward and inward breathing in the nostrils made equal; own senses, mind, and reason held in check, rid of longing, fear and wrath and intent on freedom.

29. Knowing me as the Acceptor of sacrifice and austerity, the Divine of the entire world, the friend of all creation, the Yogi attains to peace.

6

Dhyan-Yog (Culmination of Congruent)

Bhagwan: Shri Krishan Said:

1. The One, who performs all obligatory action, without depending on the fruit thereof, is a Sannyasi or a Yogi, not the One, who neglects the sacrificial fire nor One, who neglects action.

2. What is called Sannyas, know thou to be Yog, dear Pandav; for none can become a Yogi who has not renounced selfish purpose.

3. For the person, who seeks to scale the heights of Yog, action is said to be the means; for the same One, when One has scaled those heights, repose is said to be the means.

4. When a person is not attached either to the objects of sense or to actions and sheds all selfish purpose, then that One is said to have scaled the heights of Yog.

5. By one's Self should one raise oneself, and not allow oneself to fall for Aatma alone is the friend of self, and self alone is self's foe.

6. The One's-self alone is friend, who has conquered own-self by own-self: but to own, who has not conquered own-self and is thus inimical to own-self, even own-self behaves as foe.

7. The One, who has conquered own-self and who rests in perfect calm the self is completely composed, in cold and heat, in pleasure and pain, in honour and dishonour.

8. The Yogi who is filled with the contentment of wisdom and discriminative knowledge, who is firm as a rock, who has the supremacy over own senses, and to whom a clod of earth, a stone and gold are the same, is possessed of Yog (Able).

9. The One, who excels who regards alike the boon companion, the friend, the enemy, the stranger, the mediator,

10. Let the Yogi constantly apply his thought to Aatma remaining alone in a scheduled place, One's mind and body in control, rid of desires and possessions.

11. Fixing for own-self, in a pure spot, a firm seat, neither too high nor yet too low, but not covered with Kusha (grass), or a thereon a deerskin, even thereon a cloth;

12. Sitting on that seat, with mind concentrated, the functions of thought and sense of control, One should set own-self to the practice just to be a Yogi for the sake of self-purification.

13. Keeping own-self steady, holding the trunk, the neck and the head in a straight line and motionless, fixing own eyes on the tip of own nose, and looking not around.

14. Tranquil in spirit, free from fear, steadfast in the vow of Brahm-Acharya, holding own mind in control, as that the Yogi sits, with all own thoughts on me, absorbed in me.

15. The Yogi, who ever thus, with mind controlled, unites own-self to Aatma, wins the peace which culminates in Nirman (Existace), the peace that is in me.

16. The Yog doesn't means that One, who doesn't eats too much, nor for own who fasts too much, neither for own who sleeps too much, nor yet for own who is too wakeful.

17. The One, who is in disciplined for food and recreation, in effort in all activities, and in sleep and waking, Yog (Ability in discipline) becomes a relief from all ills.

18. When One's thought, completely controlled, rests steadily on only Aatma, when one is free from longing for all objects of desire, then One is called a Yogi.

19. As a taper in a windless spot flickers not, even so is a Yog, with own thought controlled, seeking to unite own self with Aatma (Soul).

20. Where thought curbed by the practice of Yog completely ceases, where a person sits content within own self, Aatma having seen Aatma.

21. Where One, who experiences that endless bliss beyond the senses which can be grasped by reason alone, wherein established, One swerves not from the Truth;

22. Where One, who holds no other gain greater than that which One has gained; and where, securely seated, tat One is not shaken by any calamity however great.

23. That state should be known as Yog (attachment with the Supreme), the disunion from all union with pain. This Yog must one practice with firm resolve and unwearying zeal.

24. Shaking oneself completely free from longings born of selfish purpose; reining in the whole host of senses, from all sides, with the mind itself;

25. With reason held securely by the Will, that One should gradually attain calm and with the mind established in Aatma think of nothing.

26. Wherever the fickle and unsteady mind wanders, thence should it be reined and brought under the sole sway of Aatma.

28. The Yogi, cleansed of all stain, unites himself ever thus to Aatma, easily enjoys the endless bliss of contact with Brahm.

29. The One, who equipped with Yog looks on all with an impartial eyes, seeing Aatma in all beings and all beings in Aatma.

30. The One, who sees me everywhere and everything in me, never vanishes from me nor I from that One.

31. The Yogi, who, anchored in unity, worships me abiding in all beings, lives and moves in me, no matter how that Ones live and move.

32. The One, who, by likening own-self with others, senses pleasure and pain equally for all as for own-self, is deemed to be the highest Yog, dear Arjun.

Arjun Said:

33. I do not see, dear Madhusudan, how this Yog, based on the equal-mindedness that Thou hast expounded to me, can steadily endure, because of fickleness of the mind.

34. For fickle is the mind, dear Shree Krishn, unruly, overpowering and stubborn; to curb it is, I think, as hard as to curb the wind.

Bhagwan: Shree Krishan Said:

35. Undoubtedly, dear Maha-Bahu, the mind is fickle

and hard to curb, yet, dear Kaunteya, it can be held in check by constant practice and dispassion.

36. Without self-restraint, Yog, that I hold, is difficult to attain; but the self-governed Aatma (soul) can attain it by proper means, if that One strives for it.

Arjun Said:

37. If one, possessed of faith, but slack of effort, because of that One's mind straying from Yog, reach not perfection in Yog, what end does One come to, dear Shree Krishn?

38. Do they not perish like a dispersing cloud, dear Shree Krishn, having lost both the heavenly and the worldly pleasures, support less and bewildered on the path of Self-realization?

39. This my doubt, dear Krishan, do thou dispel utterly; for there is to be found none other than thou to banish this doubt.

Bhagwan: Shree Krishan Said:

40. Neither in this world, nor in the next, can there be ruin for that One, dear Parth; no well-doer, dear loved one, meets with a sad end.

41. Fallen from Yog, a person attains the world of righteous souls, and having dwelt there for numberless years is then born in a house of pure and gentle blood.

42. That One may even be born into a Yogi-family, though such birth as this is all too rare in this world.

43. There, dear Kunti-Nandan, that One discovers the intellectual stage that One had reached in previous birth, and thence that One stretches forward again towards perfection.

44. By virtue of that previous practice that One is borne on, whether that One will it or not, even that One with a desire to know Yog passes beyond the Vedic ritual.

45. But the Yogi who perseveres in One's striving, cleansed of sin, perfected through many births, reaches the highest state.

46. The Yogi is deemed higher than the One's of austerities; that One is deemed also higher than that One of knowledge; higher is One's than that One engrossed in ritual; therefore be thou a Yogi, dear Arjun!

47. And among all Yogi, that One who worships me with faith, One's inmost self all rapt in me, is deemed by me to be the best Yogi.

7
Knowledge of the Almighty

Bhagwan: Shree Krishan Said:

1. Hear, dear Parth, how, with thy mind riveted on me, by practicing Yog and making me the Aatma refuge, thou shall, without doubt, know me fully.

2. I will declare to thee, in its entirety, this knowledge, combined with discriminative knowledge, which when thou hast known there remains here nothing more to be known.

3. Among thousands of person hardly one strives after perfection; among those who strive hardly one knows me in truth.

4. Earth, Water, Fire (Sun), Air (Wau-Mandle), Ether, Mind, Reason and Ego, thus eightfold is my prakriti (environment) divided.

5. This is my lower aspect; but know thou my other aspect, the higher which is jiva the Vital Essence) by which, dear Maha-Bahu, this world is sustained.

6. Know that these two compose the source from which all beings spring, I am the origin and end of the entire universe.

7. There is nothing higher than me, dear Dhananjay; all this is strung on me as a row of gems upon a thread.

8. In water I am the savour, dear Kaunteya; in the sun and the moon I am the light; the syllable Aum in all the Ved; the sound in ether, and person-ness in person.

9. I am the sweet fragrance in earth; the brilliance in fire; the life in all beings; and the austerity in ascetics.

10. Know me, dear Parth, to be the primeval seed of all beings; I am the reason of rational beings and the splendour of the splendid.

11. Of the strong, I am the strength, divorced from lust and passion; in beings I am desire un-divorced from righteousness.

12. Know that all the manifestations of the three Gun: Satyo-Gun, Rajo-Gun, and Tamo-Gun, proceed from none but me; yet I am not in them; they are in me.

13. Befogged by these manifestations of the three Gun, the entire world fails to recognize me, the imperishable, as transcending them.

14. For this my Divine delusive mystery made up of the three Gun is hard to pierce; but those who make me their (Aatma soul) refuge pierce the veil.

15. The deluded evil-doers, lowest of person, do not see refuge in me for, by reason of this delusive mystery, they are bereft of knowledge and given to devilish ways.

16. Four types of virtuous ones worship or seek me, dear Arjun. They are: The distressed, the seeker of Self-knowledge, the seeker of wealth, and the enlightened one who has experienced the Supreme Being.

17. Of these the enlightened, ever attached to me in single-minded devotion, is the best for to the

enlightened I am exceedingly dear and that One is dear to me.

18. All these are estimable indeed, but the enlightened I hold to be my very self for one's, the best Yogi, is stayed on me alone, the Supreme goal.

19. At the end of many births the enlightened person finds refuge in me, rare indeed is this great soul to whom myself is all.

20. The One, bereft of knowledge by reason of various longings, seek refuge in other Dev-Aatma, pinning their faith on diverse rites, guided by their own nature.

21. Whatever form one desires to worship in faith and devotion, in that very form I make that faith of One's secure.

22. Possessed of that faith the One, who seeks a propitiate that one, and obtains there through Thy longings, dispensed in truth by none but me.

23. But limited is the fruit that falls to those short-sighted ones; those who worship the Dev-Aatma (Saints) go to the Dev-Aatma, those who worship me come unto me.

24. Not knowing my transcendent, imperishable, supreme character, the undiscerning think me who am un-manifest to have become manifest.

25. Veiled by the delusive mystery created by my unique power, I am not manifest to all; this bewildered world does not recognize me, birth-less and changeless.

26. I know, dear Arjun, all creatures past, present and to be but no one knows me.

27. All creatures in this universe are bewildered, dear Parantap, by virtue of the delusion of the pairs of opposite sprung from likes and dislikes, dear Bharat.

28. But those virtuous person whose sin has come to an end, freed from delusion and of the pairs of opposites, worship me in steadfast faith.

29. Those who endeavour for freedom from life and death by taking refuge in me, know in full that Brahm, Adhy-Aatma and all Karm.

30. The sense is that every nook and cranny of the universe is filled with Brahm, that One is the sole Agent of all the actions, and that person, who imbued to becomes one at a time of passing hence. All that one's desires are extinguished in one's vision of One's and that One wins one's freedom.

8
Attaining the Supreme

Arjun Said:

1. What is that Brahm? What is Adhy Aatma? What Karm, Purushottam? What is called Adhibhuta? And what Adhi-Dev?

2. And who here in this body is Adhiyajna and how? And how at the time of death art Thou to be known by the self-controlled?

Bhagwan: Shree Krishan Said:

3. The Supreme, the Imperishable is Brahm; its manifestation is Adhy-Aatma; the creative process whereby all beings are created is called Karm.

4. Adhibhuta is My perishable form; Adhidaivata is the individual self in that form; and best among the embodied, Adhiyajna am I in this body, purified by sacrifice.

5. Adhibhuta is my perishable form; Adhidaivata is the individual self in that form; and that best among the embodied, Adhiyajna am I in this body, purified by sacrifice the body, enters into me of that there is no doubt.

6. Whatever form a person continually contemplates,

that same One remembers in the hour of death, and to that very form One goes, dear Kaunteya.

7. Therefore at all times remember me and fight on; thy mind and reason thus on me fixed thou shall surely come to me.

8. With thought steadied by constant practice, and wandering nowhere, One, who meditates on the Supreme Celestial Being, dear Parth, goes to one's.

10. Whose, at the time of death, with unwavering mind, with devotion, and fixing the breath rightly between the brows by the power of Yog, meditates on the Sage, the Ancient, the ruler, subtler than the subtlest, the Supporter of all, the Inconceivable, glorious as the sun beyond the darkness, that One goes to that Supreme Celestial Beings.

11. That which the knower of the Ved call the Imperishable, wherein the ascetics freed from passion enter and desiring which they practice Brahm-Acharya, that Goal I will declare to thee in brief.

12. Closing all the doors, locking up the mind in the hridaya (Heart) fixing one's breath within the head, rapt in Yog (Ability) meditation;

13. Whoso departs leaving the body uttering on Hari-Oum in one syllable repeatedly thinking on me, that One reaches the highest state.

14. That Yogi easily wins to me, dear Parth, who, ever attached to me, constantly remembers me with undivided mind.

15. Great souls, having come to me, reach the highest perfection; they come not again to birth, un-lasting and an abode of misery.

16. From the world of Brahm down, all the world are subject to return, dear Arjun; but on coming to me there is no rebirth.

17. Those person indeed know what is Day and what is Night, who know that Brahm's day lasts a thousand Yug (centuries) and that one's night too is a thousand Yug long.

18. At the coming of Day all the manifest spring forth from the Un-manifest, and at the coming of night they are dissolved into that same un-manifest.

19. This same multitude of creatures come to birth, dear Parth, again and again; they are dissolved at the coming of night, whether they will or not; and at the break of Day they are re-born.

20. But higher than the Un-manifest is another Un-manifest Being, everlasting, which perisheth not when all creatures perish.

21. This Un-manifest, named the Imperishable, is declared to be the highest goal. For those who reach it there is no return. That is my highest abode.

22. This Supreme Being, dear Parth, may be won by undivided devotion; in It all beings dwell, by It all is pervaded.

23. Now I will tell thee, Bharat-Arshabha, the conditions which determine the exemption from return, as also the return, of Yogi after they pass away hence.

24. Fire, Light, Day, the Bright Fortnight, the six months of the Northern Solstice through these departing people knowing Brahm go to Brahm.

25. Smoke, Night, the Dark Fortnight, the six months of the Southern Solstice There through the Yogi attains to the lunar light and thence returns.

26. These two paths bright and dark are deemed to be the eternal paths of the world by a person goes to return not, by the other one's returns again.

27. The Yogi knowing these two paths falls not into delusion, dear Parth therefore, at all times, dear Arjun, remain steadfast in Yog.

28. Whatever fruit of good deeds is laid down as accruing from a study of the Ved, from sacrifices, austerities, and acts of charity all that the Yogi transcends, on knowing this, and reaches the Supreme and Primal Abode.

9

The Utmost Confidential Knowledge

Bhagwan: Shree Krishan Said:

1. I will now declare to thee, who art un-censorious, this mysterious knowledge, together with discriminative knowledge, knowing which thou shall be released from ill.

2. This is the king of sciences, the king of mysteries, pure and sovereign, capable of direct comprehension, the essence of Dharm (System to live), easy to practice, changeless.

3. The One's who have no faith in this doctrine, dear Parantap, far from coming to me return repeatedly to the path of this world of death.

4. By me un-manifest in form, this whole world is pervaded; all beings are in me, I am not in them.

5. And yet those beings are not in me. That indeed is my unique power as the Divine sustainers of all beings, I am not in them; my-self brings them into existence.

6. As the mighty wind, moving everywhere, is ever contained in ether, even so know that all beings are contained in me.

7. All beings, dear Kaunteya, merge into my prakriti, at the end of a period (kalpa), and I send them forth again when a period (kalpa) begins.

8. Resorting to my prakriti, I send forth again and again this multitude of beings, powerless under the sway of prakriti.

9. But all this activity, dear Dhananjaya, does not bind me, seated as one indifferent, unattached to it.

10. With me as Presiding Witness, prakriti gives birth to all that moves and does not move; and because of this, dear Kaunteya, the wheel of the world keeps going on and on.

11. Not knowing my transcendent nature as the sovereign Supreme of all beings, fools condemn me incarnated as a person.

12. Vain are the hopes, actions and knowledge of those witless ones who have resorted to the delusive nature of monsters and devils.

13. But those great souls who resort to the Divine nature, dear Parth, know me as the imperishable Source of all beings and worship me with an undivided mind.

14. Always declaring my Glory, striving in steadfast faith, they do me devout homage; ever attached to me, they worship me.

15. Yet others, with knowledge-sacrifice, worship me, who am to be seen everywhere, as one, as different or as many.

16. I am the sacrificial vow, I am the sacrifice, I the ancestral oblation, I the herb, I the sacred text, I the clarified butter, I the fire, I the burnt offering.

17. Of this universe I am the Father, Mother, Creator, Grandsire, I am what is to be known, the sacred

syllable Aum, the Rig-Ved the Sam-Ved and the Yajus-Ved.

18. I am the Goal, the Sustainers, the Supreme, the Witness, the Abode, the Refuge, the Friend; the Origin, the End the Preservation, the Treasure house, the imperishable Seed.

19. I give heat, I hold back and pour forth rain, I am deathlessness and also death. dear Arjun, Being and not Being as well.

20. Followers of the three-Ved, who drink the som-rus (juice) and are purged of sin, worship me with sacrifice and pray for going to heaven; they reach the holy world of the Thy-Glory and enjoy in heaven the Divine joys of the Divine.

21. They enjoy the vast world of heaven, and their merit spent, they enter the world of the mortals; thus those who, following the Vedic-law, long for the fruit of their action earn but the round of birth and death.

22. As for those who worship me, thinking on me alone and nothing else, ever attached to me, I bear the burden of getting them what they need.

23. Even those who, devoted to other Devta (Saints), worship them in full faith, even they, dear Kaunteya, worship none but me, though not according to the rule.

24. For I am the Acceptor and the Director of all sacrifices; but not recognizing me as I am, they go astray.

25. Those who worship the Devta (Saints) go to the saints; those who worship the spirits go to the spirits; but those who worship me come to me.

26. Any offering of leaf, flower, fruit or water, made to me in devotion, by an earnest soul, I lovingly accept.

27. Whatever thou doest, whatever thou eats, whatever thou offer as sacrifice or gift, whatever austerity thou dost perform, dear kaunteya, dedicate all to me.

28. So doing thou shall be released from the bondage of action, yielding good and evil fruit; having accomplished both renunciation and performance, thou shall be released from birth and death and come unto me.

29. I am the same to all beings; with me there is non disfavoured, none favoured; but those who worship me with devotion are in me and I in them.

30. A sinner, howsoever great, if the One, who turns to me with undivided devotion, must indeed be counted a Devta (Saints); for that One has a settled resolve.

31. Sooner the One becomes righteous and wins everlasting peace; know for a certainty, dear kaunteya, that my Bhakti (Worship) never perishes.

32. For finding refuge in me, even those who though are born of the womb of sin, women, vaishya, and shoodr too, reach the supreme goal.

33. How much more then, the pure Brahm and seer-kings who are my devotees? Do thou worship me, therefore, since thou hast come to this fleeting and joyless world.

34. On me fix thy mind, to me bring thy devotion, to me offer thy sacrifice, to me make Thy obeisance; thus having attached Thyself to me and made me thy end and aim, to me indeed shall thou come.

10
The Enjoyments of the Thee-Divine

Bhagwan: Shree Krishan Said:

1. Yet once more, dear Maha-Bahu, here my supreme word, which I will utter to thee, gratified one, for thy benefit.

2. Neither the Devta (Saints) nor the great seers know my origin; for I am, every way, the origin of them both.

3. The One, who knows me, the great Divine of the world, as birth less and without the beginning, that One among mortals, un-deluded, is released from sins.

4. Discernment, knowledge, freedom from delusion, long suffering, truth, self-restraint, inward calm, pleasure, pain, birth, death, fear and fearlessness;

5. Non-violence, even-mindedness, contentment, austerity, beneficence, good and ill fame, all these various attributes of creatures proceed verily from me.

6. The seven great seers, the ancient four, and the Manu too were born of me and of my mind, and of them were born all the creatures in the world.

7. The One, who knows in truth my immanence and my Yog becomes gifted with unshakable Yog; of this there is no doubt.

8. I am the source of all, all proceeds from me; knowing this, the wise worship me with hearts full of devotion. The great Saints, Sages, and all the creatures of the world were born from potential energy.

9. With me in their thoughts, their whole soul devoted to me, teaching one another with me ever on their lips, they live in contentment and joy.

10. To these, ever in tune with me worshipping me with affectionate devotion, I give the power of selfless action, whereby they come to me.

11. Out of every compassion for them, I who dwell in their hearts, destroy the darkness, born of ignorance, with the refulgent lamp of knowledge.

Arjun Said:

12. Divine! Thou art the Supreme Brahm, the Supreme Abode, the supreme Purifier! Everlasting Celestial Being, the Primal Devta, Unborn, All pervading.

13. Thus have all the seers the divine seer Narad, Asita, Deval, Vyas declared Thee; and Thou Thy-self dost tell me so.

14. All that Thou tell me is true, I know, dear Keshav, verily, Devine, neither the Devta nor the demons know Thy manifestation.

15. Thyself alone Thou know by Thyself, dear Purushottam, the source and Divine of all beings, Devta of all the Devta, the Ruler of the universe.

16. Indeed Thou ought to tell me of all Thy manifestations, without a remainder, whereby Thou dost pervade the world.

17. Dear Yogi! constantly meditating on Thee, how am I to know Thee? In what various aspects am I to think of Thee, dear Shree Krishan?

18. Recount to me yet again, in full detail, Thy unique power and Thy immanence, dear Janardan! For my ears cannot be sated with listening to Thy life-giving words.

Bhagwan: Shree Krishan Said:

19. Yes, I will unfold to thee, dear Bharat, my divine manifestations, the chief only for there is no limit to their extent.

20. I am the Aatma, Gudakesh, seated in the heart of every being; I am the beginning, the middle and the end of all beings.

21. Of the Adityas I am Vishnu; of luminaries, the radiant Sun of Moorat (Fotm), I am reflection of constellations of the moon.

22. Of the Ved I am the Sama-Ved; of the Inder-Dev; of the senses I am the mind of beings I am the consciousness.

23. Of Rudr I am Shankar of Yakshas and Rakshasas Kubera; of Vasus I am the Fire of mountains Meru.

24. Of priests, dear Parth, know me to be the chief Brihaspati; of army captains I am Kartikeya; and of water the ocean.

25. Of the great seers I am Bhrigu; of words I am the one syllable Aum; of sacrifices I am the Jap sacrifice; of things immovable, the Himalaya.

26. Of all trees I am Ashvattha; of the divine seers, Narad; of the heavenly choir I am Chitraratha; of the perfected I am Kapil the ascetic.

27. Of horses, Know me to be the Uchaihshravas born with Amrit; of mighty elephants I am Airavata; of people, the monarch.

28. Of weapons, I am Vajr of cows, Kamadhenu; I am Kandarpa, the Devta of generation; of serpents I am Vasuki.

29. Of cobras I am Anata; of water-dwellers I am Varun; of the manes I am Aryan and of the chastisers, Yam.

30. Of demons I am Prahlad of beckoners, the time; of beasts I am the lion; and of birds, Garud.

31. Of cleansing agents I am the Wind; of wielders of weapons, Ram of fishes I am the crocodile; of rivers the river Ganga.

32. Of creations I am the beginning, end and middle, dear Arjun; of sciences, the science of spiritual knowledge; of ebaters, the right argument.

33. Of letters, the letter A, of compounds I am the dvandva, I am the imperishable time, I am the creator to be seen everywhere.

34. All-seizing Death am I, as the source of things to be in feminine virtues I am Kirti (Glory), Shree (beauty), Vak (speech), Smriti (memory), Medha (intelligence), Dhriti (constancy) and Kshama (forgiveness).

35. Of Samna hymns I am Brihat Samna; of metres, Gayatri; of months I am Margashirsh; of seasons, the spring.

36. Of deceivers I am the dice-play; of the splendid the splendour; I am victory, I am resolution, I am the goodness of the good.

37. Of Vrishnis I am Vasudev; of Pandav-Dhananjaya; of ascetics I am Vyas; and of seers, Ushanas.

38. I am the rod of those that punish; the strategy of those seeking victory; of secret things I am silence, and the knowledge of those that know.

39. Whatever is the seed of every being, dear Arjun, that am I; there is nothing, whether moving or fixed, that can be without me.

40. there is no end to my Divine manifestations; what extent of them I have told thee now is only by way of illustration.

41. Whatever is glorious, beautiful and mighty know thou that all such has issued from a fragment of my splendour.

42. But why need thou to learn this at great length, dear Arjun? With but a part of myself I stand upholding this universe.

11

The Universal Enlighten-Form

Arjun Said:

1. Out of Thy grace towards me, thou hast told me the supreme mystery revealing the knowledge of the Supreme; it has banished my delusion.

2. Of the origin and destruction of beings I have heard from Thee in full detail, as also Thy imperishable Ajesty, dear Kamala-Patraksh!

3. Thou art indeed as Thou hast described Thyself, Parameshvar! I do crave to behold, now, that form of as Ishvar.

4. If, Thy Glory, thou think it possible for me to bear the sight, reveal to me, dear Yogeshvar, Thy imperishable form.

Bhagwan: Shee Krishan Said:

5. Behold, dear Parth my forms Divine in their unaccountable, infinitely diverse, infinitely various in colour and aspect.

6. Behold the Aditya, the Vasus, the Rudra, the two Ashwins, the Maruts; behold, dear Bharat, numerous marvels never revealed before.

7. Behold today, dear Gudakesha, in my body, the whole universe, moving and unmoving, all in one, and whatever else thou crave to see.

8. But Thou canst not see me with these own eyes. I give thee the eye Divine, behold my sovereign power!

Sanjay Said:

9. With these words, dear King, the great Divine of Yog, Hari, then revealed to Parth Thy-Supreme form as Ishvar.

10. With many mouths and many eyes, many wondrous aspects, many Divine ornaments, and many brandished weapons Divine.

11. Wearing Divine garlands and vestments, anointed with Divine perfumes, it was the form of Devta, all-marvellous infinite, seen everywhere.

12. Were the splendour of a thousand Sun to shoot forth all at once in the sky that might perchance resemble the splendour of that Mighty.

13. Then did Pandav see the whole universe in its manifold divisions gathered as one in the body of that Devta of all the Devta.

14. Then dear Dhananjay, wonderstruck and thrilled in every fibre of his being, bowed low his head before the Divine addressing thee thus with folded hands.

Arjun Said:

15. With Thy form, of Thy-Glory, I see all the Devta and the diverse multitudes of beings, the Brahm, on Thy lotus-throne and all the seers and serpents Divine.

16. With many arms and bellies, mouths and eyes, I see Thy infinite form everywhere. Neither Thy-end, nor

middle, nor beginning, do I see, Thy-Glory of the Universe, in the Universal-formed!

17. With crown and mace and disc, a mass of effulgence, gleaming everywhere I see Thee, so dazzling to the sight, bright with the splendour of the fiery sun blazing from all sides, incomprehensible.

18. Thou art the Supreme Imperishable worthy to be known; Thou art the final resting place of this universe; Thou art the changeless guardian of the Eternal Dharam; Thou art, I believe, the Everlasting Being.

19. Thou hast no beginning, middle nor end; infinite is Thy might; arms innumerable; for eyes, the sun and the moon; Thy mouth a blazing fire, overpowering the universe with Thy radiance.

20. By Thee alone are filled the spaces between heaven and earth and all the quarters; at the sight of this Thy wondrous terrible form, the three world are sore oppressed, dear Mahatma!

21. Here, too, the multitudes themes of form are seen to enter Thee; some awe-struck praise Thee with folded arms; the hosts of great seers and Siddh, 'All Hail' on their lips, hymn Thee with songs of praise.

22. The Rudr, Aditya, Vasus, Sadhya, all the Devta, the twin Ashwins, Marut, the hosts of Gandharv, Yaksha, Asur and Siddh all gaze on Thee in wonderment.

23. At the sight of Thy-Mighty form, dear Maha-Bahu, many-mouthed, with eyes, arms, thighs and feet innumerable, with many vast bellies, terrible with many jaws, the worlds feel fearfully oppressed, and so do I.

24. For as I behold Thee touching the sky, glowing, numerous-hued with gaping mouths and wide

resplendent eyes, I feel oppressed in my innermost being; no peace nor quiet I find, dear Vishnu!

25. As I see Thy mouths with fearful jaws, resembling the Fire of Doom, I lose all sense of direction, and find no relief. Be gracious, Devesh, Jagan-Niwss (Glowing Haven).

26. All the sons of king Dhritarashtr, and with them the crowd of Bhishm, Dron, and that Karn too, as also our chief warriors.

27. Are hastening into the fearful jaws of Thy terrible mouths. Some indeed, caught between Thy teeth, are seen, their heads being crushed to atoms.

28. As rivers, in their numerous torrents, run head-long to the sea, even so the heroes of the world of people rush into Thy flaming mouths.

29. As moths, fast-flying, plunge into blazing fire, straight to their doom, even so these rush headlong into Thy mouths, to their destruction.

30. Devouring all these from all sides, Thou lap them with Thy flaming tongues; Thy fierce rays blaze forth, filling the whole universe with their lustre.

31. Tell me, Thy-Glory, who Thou art so dread of form! Hail to Thee, Dev Be gracious! I desire to know Thee, Primal Glory; for I comprehend not what Thou dost.

Bhagwan: Shree Krishan Said:

32. Doom am I, full-ripe, dealing death to the worlds, engaged in devouring human beings. Even without slaying them not one of the warriors, ranged for battle against thee, shall survive.

33. Therefore, do thou arise, and win renown! Defeat thy foes and enjoy a thriving kingdom. By me have these

already been destroyed; be thou no more than an instrument, Savyasachin!

34. Drona, Bhishm, Jayadrath and Karn, as also the other warrior chiefs already slain by me slay thou! Fight! Victory is over the foes in the field.

Sanjay Said:

35. Hearing this world of Keshav, crown-wearer Arjun folded his hands, and trembling made obeisance. Bowing and all hesitant, in faltering accents, he proceeded to address Shree Krishn once more.

Arjun Said:

36. Right proper it is, dear Hrishikesh, that Thy praise should stir the world to gladness and tender emotion; the Rakshas in fear fly to every quarter and all the hosts of Siddh do reverent homage.

37. And why should they not bow down to Thee, dear Mahatma? Thou art the First Creator, greater even than Brahm. Dear Anant, dear Devesh, dear Jagannivas, Thou art the Imperishable, Being, not-Being, and That which transcends even these.

38. Thou art the Primal Supreme, the Ancient Being, Thou art the Final Resting Place of this Universe; Thou art the Knower, the to be known the Supreme Abode by Thee, dear Myriad-formed, is the universe pervaded.

39. Thou art Vayu, Yam, Agni, Varun, Shashank, Prajapati, and Prapitamah! All Hail to Thee, an endless times all hail! Again and yet again all hail to Thee!

40. All hail to Thee from before and behind! all hail to Thee from every side, dear All. Thy prowess is infinite,

Thy-Might is measureless! Thou hold all; therefore Thou art all.

41. If ever in carelessness, thinking of Thee as comrade, I addressed Thee saying, dear Yadav not knowing Thy greatness, in negligence or in affection,

42. If ever I have been rude to Thee in jest, whilst at play, at rest-time, or at meals, whilst alone or in company, dear Achyuta, forgive Thou my fault I beg of Thee, Incomprehensible!

43. Thou art Father of this world, of the moving and the un-moving; Thou art its adored, its worthiest, supper; there is none equal to Thee; how then any greater than Thee? Thy power is matchless in the three world.

44. Therefore, I prostrate myself before Thee, and beseech Thy grace, Thy-Glory adorable! As father with son, as comrade with comrade, so should Thou bear, beloved Glory, with me, Thy loved one.

45. I am filled with joy to see what never was seen before, and yet my heart is oppressed with fear. Show me that original form of Thine Glory! Be gracious, Devesh, Jagan-Niwas!

46. I crave to see Thee even as Thou enormous, with crown, with mace, and disc in hand; wear Thou, once more, that four-armed form, dear thousand-armed Vishv-Murti!

Bhagwan: Shree Krishan Said:

47. It is to favour Thee, dear Arjun, that I have revealed to Thee, by My own unique power, this my form Supreme, Resplendent, Universal, Infinite, Primal which none save Thee has ever seen.

48. Not by the study of the Ved, not by sacrifice, not by the study of other scriptures, not by gifts, nor yet by

performance of rites or of fierce austerities can I, in such a form, be seen by any one save Thee in the world of people, dear Kurupravir!

49. Be thou neither oppressed nor bewildered to look on this awful form of Mine. Banish Thy fear, ease thy mind, and lo! behold me once again as I was.

Sanjay Said:

50. So said Vasudev to Arjun, and revealed to own once more Own original form. Wearing again His form benign, the Mahatma consoled him terrified.

Arjun Said:

51. Beholding again Thy benign human form I am come to myself and once more in my normal state.

Bhagwan: Shree Krishan Said:

52. Very hard to behold is that form of Mine which Thou hast seen; even the Devta-jan, (Saints) always yearn to see me.

53. Not by the Ved, not by penance, nor by gifts, nor yet by sacrifice, can any behold me in the form that Thou hast seen.

54. But by single-minded devotion, dear Arjun, I may in this form be known and seen, and realisably entered into, dear Parantap!

55. The One, who alone comes to me, dear Pandav, who does my work, who has made me the goal, who is my devotee, who has renounced attachment, who has ill-will toward none.

12

Devotional Service (Bhakti-Yog)

Arjun Said:

1. Of the devotees who thus worship Thee, incessantly attached, and those who worship the Imperishable Un-manifest, which are the better Yogi?

Bhagwan: Shree Krishan Said:

2. Those I regard as the best Yogi who, riveting their minds on me, ever attached, worship me, with the highest faith.

3. But those who worship the Imperishable, the indefinable, the Un-manifest, the Omnipresent, the Unthinkable, the Rock-seated, the Immovable, the Unchanging.

4. Keeping the whole host of senses in complete control, looking on all with an impartial eyes, engrossed in the welfare of all beings these come indeed to me.

5. Greater is the travail of those whose mind is fixed on the Un-manifest; for it is hard for embodied mortals to gain the Un-manifest Goal.

6. But those who casting all their actions on me, making me their all in all, worship me with the meditation of undivided devotion.

7. Of such, whose thoughts are cantered on me, dear Parth, I become ere long the Deliverer from the ocean of this world of death.

8. On me set Thy mind, on me rest Thy conviction; thus without doubt shall Thou remain only in me hereafter.

9. If Thou canst not set thy mind steadily on me, then by the method of constant practice seek to win me, dear Dhananjay.

10. If thou art also unequal to this method of constant practice, concentrate on service for me; even thus serving me thou shall attain perfection.

11. If thou art unable even to do this, then dedicating all to me, with mind controlled, abandon the fruit of action.

12. Better is knowledge than practice, better than knowledge is concentration, better than concentration is renunciation of the fruit of all action, from which directly issues.

13. Who has ill-will towards none, who is friendly and compassionate, who has shed all thought of 'mine' or ' I ', who regards pain and pleasure alike, who is long-suffering.

14. Who is ever content, gifted with Yog, self-restrained, of firm conviction, who has dedicated own mind and reason to me that devotee of mine is dear to me.

15. Who gives no trouble to the world, to whom the world causes no trouble, who is free from exultation, resentment, fear and vexation, that person is dear to me.

16. Who expects naught, who is pure, resourceful, unconcerned, untroubled, who indulges in no undertakings, that devotee of mine is dear to me.

17. Who rejoices not, neither frets nor grieves, who covets not, who abandons both good and ill that devotee of mine is dear to me.

18. Who is same to foe and friend, who regards alike respect and disrespect, cold and heat, pleasure and pain, who is free from attachment.

19. Who weighs in equal scale blame and praise, who is silent, content with whatever own lot, who owns no home, who is of steady mind, that devotee of mine is dear to me.

20. They who follow this essence of Dharm, as I have told it, with faith, keeping me as their goal, those devotees are exceeding dear to me.

13

The Nature, and the Consciousness in Life

Bhagwan: Shree Krishan Said:

1. This body, dear Kaunteya, is called the Field; the One, who knows it is called the knower of the field by those who know.

2. understand me to be, dear Bharata, the knower of the field in all the fields; and the knowledge of the field and the knower of the field, I hold, is resalable knowledge.

3. What the field is, what its nature, what its modifications, and whence is what, as also who that One is, and what own power, hear this briefly from me.

4. This subject has been sung by seers distinctively and in various ways, in different hymns as also in aphoristic texts about Brahm well reasoned and unequivocal.

5. The great elements, Individuation, Reason, the Unmanifest, the ten senses, and the one mind, and the related spheres of the senses.

6. Desire, dislike, pleasure, pain, association, consciousness, cohesion this, in sum, is what is called the Field with its modifications.

7. Freedom from pride and pretentiousness, non-violence, forgiveness, uprightness, service of the skilled, purity, steadfastness, self-restraint.

8. Aversion from sense-objects, absence of conceit, realization of the painfulness and evil of birth, death, age and disease;

9. Absence of attachment, refusal to be wrapped up in one's children, wife, home and family, even-mindedness whether good or ill befall.

10. Unwavering and all-exclusive devotion to me, resort to secluded spots, distaste for the haunts of people.

11. Settled conviction of the nature of the Aatma, perception of the goal of the knowledge of reality.

12. I will now expound to thee that which is to be known and knowing which one enjoys immortality; it is the supreme Brahm (Universe) which has no beginning, which is called neither Beings nor non-Beings.

13. Everywhere having hands and feet, everywhere having eyes, heads, mouths, everywhere having ears, It abides embracing everything in the universe.

14. Seeming to possess the functions of the senses, It is devoid of all the senses. It touches naught, upholds all; having no Gun (Natural-qualities), It experiences the Gun.

15. Without all beings, immovable yet moving, so subtle that It cannot be perceived; and yet so near it is. The One, who knows It is within It, close; mobility and immobility, peace and restlessness, for It has motion and yet is motionless.

16. Undivided, It seems to subsist divided in all beings; that which is to be known as the Sustainers of all, yet It is their devourer and creator.

17. Light of all lights, It is said to be beyond darkness; It is knowledge, the object of knowledge, to be gained only by knowledge; It is seated in the hearts of all.

18. Thus have I expounded in brief the field, knowledge and that which is to be known; My devotee, when that One knows this, is worthy to become one with me.

19. Know that Prakriti and Purusha are both without beginning; know that all the modifications and Gun are born of Prakriti (Form of Nature).

20. Prakriti is described as the cause in the creation of effects from causes; person is described as the cause of the experiencing of pleasure and pain.

21. For the person residing in Prakriti, experiences the Gun born in Prakriti.

22. What is called in this body the Witness, the Assenter, the Sustainers, the Experience, the Great Divine and also the Supreme Aatma, is Supreme Being.

23. The One, who thus knows person and Prakriti with its Gun, is not born again, no matter how, the ones live and move.

24. Some through meditation hold the Aatma by themselves in their own self; others by Sankhy (doubt) Yog, and others by Karm-Yog (The ability of functions).

25. Yet others, not knowing The Divine's worship having heard from others; they too pass beyond death, because of devoted adherence to what they have heard.

26. Wherever something is born, animate or inanimate, know thou Bharat-arshabh, that it issues from the union of the field and the knower of the field.

27. Who sees abiding in all beings the same Param-Ishvar, imperishable in the perishable, that One sees indeed.

28. When that One sees the same Ishvar abiding everywhere alike, that One does not hurt own-self by that One-self and hence that One attains the highest goal.

29. Who sees that it is Prakriti that performs all actions and thus knows that Aatma performs them not, that One sees indeed.

30. When that One sees the diversity of beings as founded in unity and the whole expanse issuing there from, then that One attains to Brahm.

31. This imperishable Supreme Aatma, dear Kaunteya, though residing in the body, acts not and is not stained, for that One has no beginning and no Gun (Natural qualities).

32. As the all-pervading ether, by reason of its subtlety, is not soiled even so Aatma pervading every part of the body is not soiled.

33. As the one Sun illumines the whole universe, even so the Supreme of the field illumines the whole field, dear Bharat!

34. Those who, with the eyes of knowledge, thus perceive the distinction between the field and the Knower of the field, and the secret of the release of beings from Prakriti, they attain to the Supreme.

14

The Main Modes of the Nature

Bhagwan: Shree Krishan Said:

1. Yet again I will expound the highest and the best of all knowledge, knowing which all the Sages passed hence to the highest perfection.

2. By having recourse to this knowledge they became one with me. They need not come to birth even at a creation, nor do they suffer at a dissolution.

3. The great prakriti is for me the womb in which I deposit the germ; from it all beings come to birth, dear Bharat.

4. Whatever forms take birth in the various species, the great prakriti is their mother and I the seed-giving father.

5. Satyo, Rajo and Tamo are the Gun sprung from prakriti; it is they, dear Maha-Bahu, that keep the imperishable dweller bound to the body.

6. Of these Satya, being stainless, is light-giving and healing; it binds with the bond of happiness and the bond of knowledge, is sinless one.

7. Rajo, know thou, is of the nature of passion, the source of thirst and attachment; it keeps that One bound with the bond of action.

8. Tamo, know thou, born of ignorance, is mortal that One's delusion; it keeps own bound with heedlessness, sloth and slumber, dear Bharat.

9. Purity attaches one to happiness, passion is caused of action, dear Arjun, but inertia by covering wisdom attaches to negligence.

10. Purity prevails, overcoming passion and inertia, dear Arjun. Passion prevail subdue purity and inertia and thus inertia prevails over pawing purity and passion.

11. When the light of knowledge spreads through all the passages of the body, then it is known that the purity has increased.

12. Avarice activity, initiative restlessness and desires, result from the increase and desires, result it from the increase in the Rajo-Gun, dear Best among the brothers.

13. Darkness, slothfulness, negligence and delusion these are caused by the increase of inertia or indolence inducing Tamo-Gun, dear Arjun.

14. When the self is dissolved, when the goodness becomes predominant then it reaches to the world of purity of those, who have known the Heaven (Brahm-lok).

15. When passion becomes predominant at the time of dissolution, it is born in the world of those attached to activities and if it is dissolved when dullness or inertia is overpowering quality, it is born into the womb of the ignorant.

16. The results of the good action is said to be of the quality of goodness and purity, while the passion causes pain and ignorance is the fruit of inertia.

17. Knowledge is resulted from purity, passion gives rise

to avarice ignorance and delusion are caused by inertia as also erroneous action.

18. Who are set in goodness rise upwards the passionate remain in the middle regions the inert involved in.

19. When the sage perceived factor other than modes of Gun, and also knows what is beyond the modes of Gun (qualities) that one attains to my form.

20. When the self roars above these three qualities arising from the body, it goes beyond birth, death, decay and pain and reaches the state of permanent blissfulness when there is no birth or death.

Arjun Said:

21. Dear Kashiv, when the signs can be known that who has gone beyond the three qualities (Gun)? How does one live? How does one manage to reach beyond the modes of Gun?

Shree Krishan Said:

22. Dear Arjun, the ones, who do not abhor illumination, activity and delusion when they spring, nor crave for them when they cease to exist.

23. The ones, who sitting unconcernedly, without being disturbed by the modes or qualities (Gun), who stands aloof, without faltering, knowing that it is the modes that act and react.

24. The ones, who treat pleasure and pain similarly, who is established in one self, who regards a dud, a stone and piece of gold as of equal value, whose mind is even amidst things pleasant or unpleasant, firm of mind.

25. Who holds alike respect and disrespect, who is the same to friend and foe, who indulges in no

undertakings, that One is called Gunwan (Full of natural qualities).

26. The One, who serves me in an unwavering and exclusive Bhagti-Yog transcends these Gun and is worthy to become one with Brahm (Universe).

27. For I am the very image of Brahm, changeless and deathless, as also of everlasting Dharam (Functions of Thy-Glory within every living beings) and perfect bliss.

15
The Yog of Supreme

Bhagwan: Shree Krishan Said:

1. With the root above and branches below, the Ashvattha tree, they say, is impossible; it has Vedic hymns for its leaves; the One, who knows it knows the Ved.

2. Above all and below its branches spread, blossoming because of the Gun, having for their shoots the sense-objects; deep down in the world of people are ramified its roots, in the shape of the consequences of action.

3. Its form as such is not here perceived, neither is its end, nor beginning, nor basis. Let the One first hew down this deep-rooted Ashvattha with the sure weapon of detachment;

4. Let that One pray to win to that haven from which there is no return and seek to find refuge in the primal being from whom has emanated this ancient world of action.

5. To that imperishable haven those enlightened Aatma (soul) goes, that One, who are without pride and delusion, who have triumphed over the taints of attachment, who are ever in tune with the Supreme, whose passions have died, who are exempt from the pairs of opposites, such as pleasure and pain.

6. Neither the sun, nor the moon, nor fire illumine it; the One, who arrive there return not that is my supreme abode.

7. As part indeed of myself which has been the eternal beings in this world of life, attracts the mind and the senses from their place in prakriti.

8. When the supreme of the body acquires a body and discards it he carries these with own wherever that One goes, even as the wind carries scents from flower beds.

9. Having settled that One-self in the senses ears, eyes, touch, taste, and smell as well as the mind, through them that One frequents their objects.

10. The deluded perceive Thy-Glory not as the One leaves or settles in a body or enjoys sense objects in association with the Gun; it is those endowed with the eyes of knowledge who alone see Thy-Glory.

11. Yog, who strive see Thy-Glory seated in themselves; the witless ones who have not cleansed themselves to see Thy-Glory not, even though they strive.

12. The light in the sun which illumines the whole universe and which is in the moon and in fire that light, know thou, is Mine;

13. It is I, who penetrating the earth uphold all beings with my strength, and becoming the moon, the essence of all sap nourish all the herbs.

14. It is I who becoming the Vaishvanara fire and entering into the bodies of all that breathe, assimilate the four kinds of food with the help of the outward and the inward breaths.

15. And I am seated in the hearts of all, from me proceed memory, knowledge and the dispelling of doubts; it is

I who am to be known in all the Ved, I, the author of Ved and the knower of the Ved.

16. There are two Beings in the world: kshara (perishable) and akshara (imperishable). Kshara embraces all creatures and their permanent basis is akshara.

17. The Supreme Being is surely another called Paramatma who is the Imperishable Ishvar pervades and supports the three world.

18. Because I transcend the kshara and am also higher than the kshara, I am known in the world and in the Ved as Puru Shottam (the Highest Being).

19. The One, who, un-deluded, knows me as Puru-Shottam, knows all that One worships me with all that One's heart, dear Bharat.

20. Thus I have revealed to Thee, sinless one, this most mysterious Shastr (eternal-feelings) that One, who understands this, dear Bharat, is a person of understanding, the One has fulfilled own life's mission.

16

Thee-Divine and Demoniac Nature

Bhagwan: Shree Krishan Said:

1. Fearlessness, purity of heart, steadfastness in Yog knowledge and action beneficence, selt-restraint, sacrifice, spiritual study, austerity, and uprightness;

2. Non-violence, truth, slowness to wrath, the spirit of dedication, serenity, aversion to slander, tenderness to all that lives, freedom from greed, gentleness, modesty, freedom from levity.

3. Spiritedness, forgiveness, fortitude, purity, freedom from ill-will and arrogance these are to be found in one born with the divine heritage, dear Bharat.

4. Pretentiousness, arrogance, self-conceit, wrath, coarseness, ignorance these are to be found in one born with the devilish heritage.

5. The Divine heritage makes for Freedom, the devilish for bondage. Grieve not, dear Parth; Thou art born with a Divine heritage.

6. These are the orders of created beings in this world the Divine and the Devilish; the Divine order has been described in detail, hear from me now of the Devilish, dear Parth.

7. The Ones, who the devils do not know what they may do and what they may not do neither is there any purity, nor right conduct, nor reality to be found in them.

8. Without reality, without basis, without Supreme is the universe, they say, born of the union of the yonder (Male and female), prompted by naught but lust.

9. Holding this view, these depraved souls, of feeble understanding and of fierce deeds, come forth as enemies of the world to destroy it.

10. Given to insatiable lust, possessed by pretentiousness, arrogance and conceit, they seize wicked purposes in their delusion, and go about pledged to un-cleaned deeds.

11. Given to boundless cares that end only with their death, making indulgence or lust their sole goal, convinced that that is all.

12. Caught in a myriad snares of hope, slaves to lust and wrath, they speak unlawfully to amass wealth for the satisfaction of their appetites.

13. 'This have I gained today; this aspiration shall I now attain; this wealth is mine; this likewise shall be mine hereafter.

14. 'This enemy I have already slain, others also I shall slay, Supreme of all am I enjoyment is mine, perfection is mine, strength is mine, happiness is mine.

15. 'Wealthy am I, and high-Appearance. What other is like unto me? I shall perform a sacrifice! I shall give alms! I shall be merry!' Thus think they, by ignorance deluded.

16. And tossed about by diverse fancies, caught in the

net of delusion, stuck deep in the indulgence of appetites, into foul hell they fall.

17. Wise in their own conceit, stubborn, full of the intoxication of pelf and pride, they offer nominal sacrifices for show, contrary to the rule.

18. Given to pride, force, arrogance, lust and wrath they are deriders indeed, scorning me in their own and other' bodies.

19. These cruel scorners, lowest of mankind and vile, I hurl down again and again, into devilish wombs.

20. Doomed to devilish wombs, these deluded ones, far from ever coming to me, sink lower and lower in birth after birth.

21. These-folds are the passages of hell, leading a person to perdition Lust, Wrath, and Greed; these are, therefore, should be shunned.

22. The One, who escapes these passages of darkness, dear Kaunteya, works out for own welfare and thence reaches the highest state.

23. The One, who forsakes the rule of Shastr and does but the bidding of his selfish desires, gains neither perfection, nor happiness, nor the highest state.

24. Therefore, let Shastr (System) be Thy-authority for determining what ought to be done or what ought not to be done; ascertain Thou the rule of the Shastr and do Thy-function accordingly.

17
Thee-Divisions of Trust

Arjun Said:

1. What, then, dear Shree Krishn, is the position of those who forsake the rule of Shastr and yet worship with faith? Do they act from Satyo-Gun or Rajo Gun or Tamo Gun?

Bhagwan:Shree Krishan Said:

2. These folds are the faith of the Ones, an expression of their nature in each case; it is Satyo, Rajo or Tamo. hear Thou of it.

3. The faith of every One is in accord with the one's innate character; the One is made up of faith, whatever own object of faith, even so is the One.

4. Satyo-Gun persons worship the Supreme, Gun ones, the Yakshas and Rakshas; and others the One of Tamo-Gun worship manes and spirits.

5. Those Ones, who, wedded to pretentiousness and arrogance, possessed by the violence of lust and passion, practice fierce austerity not ordained by Shastr.

6. They, whilst they torture the several elements that make up their bodies, torture me too dwelling in them; know them to be of unholy resolves.

7. Of these kinds-Gun again is the food that is dear to each; so also are sacrifice, austerity, and charity. Hear how they differ.

8. Victuals that add to one's years, vitality, strength, health, happiness and appetite, are savoury, rich, substantial and inviting, are dear to the Satyo-Gun

9. Victuals that are bitter, sour, salty, over-hot, spicy, dry, burning, and causing pain, bitterness and disease, are dear to Rajo-Gun.

10. Food which has become cold, insipid, putrid, stale, discarded and unfit for sacrifice, is dear to the Tamo-Gun.

11. That sacrifice is Satyo-Gun which is willingly offered as a duty without desire for fruit and according to the rule.

12. But when sacrifice is offered with an eye to fruit and for vain glory, know, Bharata-Shreshtha, that it is Rajo-Gun.

13. Sacrifice which is contrary to the rule, which produces no food, which lacks the sacred text, which involves no giving up, which is devoid of faith is said to be Tamo-Gun.

14. Homage to the Devta-Jan, to Brahm, to Guru or to wise person; cleanliness, uprightness, Brahm-Acharya and non-violence these constitute austerity Tapo-Gun (Spiritually functioning) of the body.

15. Words that cause no hurt, that are true loving and helpful, and spiritual study constitute austerity of speech.

16. Serenity, benignity, silence, self-restraint, and purity of the spirit these constitute austerity of the mind.

17. This threefold austerity practiced in perfect faith by people not desirous of fruit, and disciplined, is said to be Satyo-Gun.

18. Austerity which is practiced with an eye to gain praise, honour and homage and for ostentation is said to be Rajo-Gun; it is fleeting and unstable.

19. Austerity which is practiced from any foolish obsession, either to torture oneself or to procure another's ruin, is called Tamo-Gun.

20. Charity, given as a matter of duty, without expectation of any return, at the right place and time, and to the right person is said to be Satyo-Gun.

21. Charity, which is given either in hope of receiving in return, or with a view of winning merit, or grudgingly, is declared to be Rajo-Gun.

22. Charity given at the wrong place and time, and to the undeserving recipient disrespectfully and with contempt is declared to be Tamo-Gun.

23. Aum-Satya has been pronounced to be the threefold name of Brahm and by that name were created of old the Brahm, the Ved and sacrifices.

24. Therefore, with Aum ever on their lips, are all the rites of sacrifice, charity and aus-terity, performed always to the rule, by Brahm-Vedhi (Law of Nature).

25. With the utterance of Tat (power) and without the desire for fruit are the several rites of sacrifice, austerity and charity performed by those seeking Freedom.

26. Satya (power) is employed in the sense of real and good dear Parth, Satya is also applied to beautiful deeds.

27. Constancy in sacrifice, austerity and charity, is called Satya and all work for those purposes is also Satya.

28. Whatever is done, dear Parth, by way of sacrifice, charity or austerity or any other work, is called Asatya (Fake) if done without faith. It counts for naught hereafter as here.

18

The Perfection of Renunciation

Arjun Said:

1. I wish to know the nature of renunciation and sacrifice, and the difference between the two, dear Shree Krishn.

Bhagwan: Shree Krishan Said:

2. Renunciation of actions springing from selfish desire is known as Sannyas by the seers; abandonment of the fruit of all action is called Tyag by the wise.

3. Some thoughtful persons say: 'All action should be abandoned as an evil, others say Action for sacrifice, charity and austerity should not be relinquished.

4. Hear my decision in this matter of Tyag (Renouncement), of Bharatasattam; for Tyag, too, of Mightiest of the person, has been described to be of three kinds.

5. Action for sacrifice, charity and austerity may not be abandoned; it must needs be performed. Sacrifice, charity and austerity are purifiers of the wise.

6. But even these actions should be performed abandoning all attachment and fruit; such, dear Parth, is my best and considered opinion.

7. It is not right to renounce one's allotted task, its abandonment, from delusion, is said to be Tamo-Gun.

8. The One, who abandons action, deeming it painful and for fear of straining own limbs, that One will never gain the fruit of abandonment, for own abandonment is Rajo-Gun.

9. But when an allotted task is performed from a sense of duty and with abandonment of attachment and fruit, dear Arjun, that abandonment is deemed to be Satyo-Gun.

10. Neither does he disdain unpleasant action, nor does the One's cling to pleasant action this wise person full of Satya, who practices abandonment, and who has shaken off all doubts.

11. For the embodied one cannot completely abandon action; but the One, who abandons the fruit of action is named a Tyagi (Unattached).

12. To those who do not practice abandonment accrues, when they pass away, the fruit of action which is of three kinds: disagreeable, agreeable, mixed; but never to the Sannyasi (Unattached person but apart from the essential nature).

13. Learn, from me, dear Maha-Bahu, the five factors mentioned in the Sankhayan (doubts) doctrine for the accomplishment of all action:

14. The field, the doer, the various means, the several different operations, the fifth and the last, the Unseen.

15. Whatever action, right or wrong, a person undertakes to do with the body, speech or mind, these are the five factors thereof.

16. This being so, the One, who, by reason of unenlightened intellect, sees the unconditioned Aatma as the agent such a person is dense and unseeing.

17. The One, who is free from all senses, whose motive is untainted, slays not nor is bound, even though the One slay all these world.

18. Knowledge, the object of knowledge, and the knower compose the threefold urge to action; the means, the action and the doer compose the threefold sum of action.

19. Knowledge, action, and the doer are of three kinds according to their different Gun, hear thou these, just as they have been described in the science of the Gun.

20. Know that knowledge whereby one sees in all beings immutable entity a unity in diversity to be Satyo-Gun.

21. That knowledge which perceives separately in all beings several entities of diverse kinds, know thou to be Rajo-Gun.

22. And knowledge which, without reason, clings to one single thing, as though it were everything, which misses the true essence and is superficial is Tamo-Gun.

23. That action is called Satyo-Gun which, being one's allotted task, is performed without attachment, without like or dislike, and without a desire for fruit.

24. That action which is prompted by the desire for fruit, or by the thoughts, which involves much dissipation of energy is called Rajo-Gun.

25. That action which is blindly undertaken without any regard to capacity and consequences, involving loss and hurt, is called Tamo-Gun.

26. That doer is called Satyo-Gun, the One, who has shed all attachment, all thoughts, who is filled with firmness and zeal, and who recks neither success nor failure.

27. That doer is said to be Rajo-Gun who is passionate, desirous of the fruit of action, greedy, violent, unclean, and moved by joy and sorrow.

28. That doer is called Tamo-Gun who is undisciplined, vulgar, stubborn, knavish, spiteful, indolent, woebegone, and dilatory.

29. Hear now, dear Dhananjay, detailed fully and severally, the threefold division of understanding and will, according to their Gun.

30. That understanding, dear Parth, is Satyo-Gun which knows action from inaction, what ought to be done from what ought not to be done, fear from fearlessness and bondage from release.

31. That understanding, dear Parth, is Rajo-Gun, which decides erroneously between right and wrong, between what ought to be done and what ought not to be done.

32. That understanding, dear Parth, is Tamo-Gun, which, shrouded in darkness, thinks wrong to be right and mistakes everything for its reverse.

33. That will, dear Parth, is Satya-Gun which maintains an unbroken harmony between the activities of the mind, the vital energies and the senses.

34. That will, dear Parth, is Rajo-Gun which clings, with attachment, to righteousness, desire and wealth, desirous of fruit in each case.

35. That will, dear Parth, is Tamo-Gun, whereby insensate the One does not abandon sleep, fear, grief, despair and self-conceit.

36. Hear now from me, dear Bharat, the three kinds of pleasure. Pleasure which is enjoyed only by repeated practice, and which puts an end to pain.

37. Which, in its inception, is as poison, but in the end as nectar, born of the serene realization of the true nature of Aatma that pleasure is said to be Satyo-Gun.

38. That pleasure is called Rajo-Gun which, arising from the contact of the senses with their objects, is at first as nectar but in the end like poison.

39. That pleasure is called Tamo-Gun which arising from sleep and sloth and heedlessness, stupefies the soul both at first and in the end.

40. There is no being, either on earth or in heaven among the Thy-Glory, that can be free from these three Gun born of prakriti.

41. The duties of Brahm, Kshatriyas, Vaishya, and Shudr, are distributed according to their innate qualifications, dear Parantap.

42. Serenity, self-restraint, austerity, purity, forgiveness, uprightness, knowledge and discriminative knowledge, faith in The Devie are the Brahm's natural duties.

43. Valour, spiritedness, constancy, resourcefulness, not fleeing from battle, generosity, and the capacity to rule are the natural duties of a Kshatriya.

44. Tilling the soil, protection of the cow and commerce are the natural functions of a Vaishy, while service is the natural duty of a Shudr.

45. Each person, by complete absorption in the performance of personal duty, wins perfection. Hear now how that One wins such perfection by devotion to that duty.

46. By offering the worship of Thy duty to The Divine,

the One, who is the moving spirit of all beings, and by whom all this is pervaded, the One wins perfection.

47. Better one's own duty, though uninviting, than another's which may be more easily performed; doing duty which accords with one's nature, one incurs no sin.

48. One should not abandon, dear Kaunteya, that duty to which one is born, imperfect though it be; for all action, in its inception, is enveloped in imperfection, as fire in smoke.

49. The One, who has weaned own-self of all kinds, who is master of own-self, who is dead to desire, attains through renunciation the perfection of freedom from action.

50. Learn now from me, in brief, dear Kaunteya, how the One, who has gained this perfection, attains to Brahm, the supreme consummation of knowledge.

51. Equipped with purified understanding, restraining the self with firm will, abandoning sound and other objects of the senses, putting aside likes and dislikes,

52. Living in solitude, spare in diet, restrained in speech, body and mind, ever absorbed in Dhyan-Yog, anchored in dispassion.

53. Without pride, violence, arrogance, lust, wrath, possession, having shed all sense of mine and at peace with own-self, that One is fit to become One with Brahm.

54. One with Brahm and at peace with own-self, that One grieves not, nor desires; holding all beings alike, the One achieves supreme devotion to me.

55. By devotion, he realizes in truth how great I am, who

I am; and having known me in reality the One enters into me.

56. Even whilst always performing actions, the One, who makes me that One's refuge wins, by my grace, the eternal and imperishable haven.

57. Casting, with thy mind, all actions on me, make me thy goal, and resorting to the Yog of even-mindedness fix thy thought ever on me.

58. Fixing the One's Thy thought on me, thou shall surmount all obstacles by my grace; but if possessed by the sense of me thou listen not, thou shall perish.

59. If obsessed by the sense of me, thou think, 'I will not fight', vain is thy obsession; Thy nature will compel thee.

60. What thou wilt not do, dear Kaunteya, because of thy delusion, thou shall do, even against Thy will, bound as thou art by the duty to which thou art born.

61. The Divine, dear Arjun, dwells in the heart of every being and by One's delusive mystery whirls them all, as though set on a Kla-Vidhi (machine).

62. In Thy Glory alone seek thy refuge with all thy heart, dear Bharat. By Thy grace shall Thou win to the eternal heaven of supreme peace.

63. Thus have I expounded to thee the most mysterious of all knowledge; ponder over it fully, then act as thou wilt.

64. Hear again my supreme word, the most mysterious of all; dearly beloved thou art of me, hence I desire to declare Thy welfare.

65. On me fix Thy mind, to me bring thy devotion, to me offer thy sacrifice, to me make Thy obeisance; to me

indeed shall Thou come solemn is my promise to Thee, Thou art dear to me.

66. Abandon all duties and come to me the only refuge. I will release thee from all sins; grieve not!

67. Utter this never to The Divine, who knows no austerity, has no devotion, nor any desire to listen, nor yet to Thy who scoffs at me.

68. The One, who will propound this supreme mystery to my devotees, shall, by that act of highest devotion to me, surely come to me.

69. Nor among person is there any who renders dearer service to me than the One; nor shall there be on earth any more beloved by me than any One.

70. And the person of faith, the One, who, scorning not, will but listen to it, even the One shall be released and will go to the happy world of people of virtuous deeds.

71. The faithful person, who is free from envy and who hears this, is liberated and attains the auspicious planets of the righteous.

72. Hast Thou heard this, dear Parth, with a concentrated mind? Has Thy delusion, born of ignorance, been destroyed, dear Dhananjaya?

Arjun Said:

73. Thanks to Thy grace, dear Achyuta, my delusion is destroyed, my understanding has returned. Now I stand secure, my doubts all dispelled; I will do Thy bidding.

Sanjay Said:

74. Thus did I hear this marvellous and thrilling discourse between Shree Vasudev and the great Souled Parth.

75. It was all by the Rishi: Shree Ved Vyas ji's kindness that I could listen to this Supreme and mysterious Yog as expounded by the lips of the Divine of Yog, Shree Krishan own-self.

76. Dear King, as often as I recall that marvellous and purifying discourse between Shree Keshav and Arjun, I am filled with recurring rapture.

77. And as often as I recall that marvellous form of Hari (Bhagwan), my wonder knows no bounds and I rejoice again and again.

78. Where so ever Shree Krishan, the Divine of Yog, is, and where so ever is Parth with Gandiv, there rest assured are Fortune, Victory, Prosperity, and Eternal Right.

Dharam

Philosophy to live forever by Dr. Sharma within the Enlightenment of Thy Glory........

The concept of the word Dharam is a set of spiritual principles of all living beings, which came into practice, since the human beings, first the mothers with their children and later on with male persons started to live together through their physical emotional and imaginary feelings, first into small but later on into large groups throughout the world. In the early stage they gone through various non–principle systems but ultimately with their day by day life experience they established the Dharam based upon the similar principles of the word Snatan to emphasize its great values and achievements.

The concept of the word Snatan is Eternal, i.e., Exists in all ages, for example, the core properties of Sun, Water, Earth and Air, etc., Dharam is usually translated as religion so called met mit and the concept of religion is a form of blindfold faith but instead the Dharam refers to our fundamental essential nature. As the Dharam for Sun is to provide light and heat throughout the planet indiscriminately, so the Dharam of all living beings is to serve each other on the same principles, for example, the Dharam of mothers or fathers is to feed and look after their children,
of mothers or fathers is to feed and look after their children,

of doctors is to serve their patients, of soldiers is to serve their countries, of kings–queens or presidents is to serve their people as we are all serving the fundamental needs of our bodies.

Our everyday way of life teaches everyone the duties and responsibilities we must uphold according to our relationship, status or occupation in life. For someone to be a son, daughter, doctor, king, queen, president, etc., must follow the Dharam inherent with that position. Thus Dharam is a wonderful synthesis of mystic philosophy and practical application in everyday life. Dharam also teaches a non sectarian appreciation which raises the worshipper to pure love for the Supreme. The characteristics of Dharam related to the way of life, are tolerance of race and non violence, detachment from the fever of material acquisition and self satisfaction through inner devotion to the creator of all living beings. Whenever the temptation of our social stratification alludes us from the principles of Dharam, then we are unable to fulfill our pure love and duties to the Supreme.

Dharam is not however, merely a set of article of faith. As a matter of fact, the Dharm is the eternal function of the Devine within every living beings while the articles of faith, belief or religion are related to the social organizations. As the needs of the society change, the articles of faith are reinterpreted to suit the changing conditions of the society, thus the articles of faith or belief or religions have been changing time and again but such changes have never ever violated the continuity of the fundamental principles of the Dharam as the highest ideal, for instance, the kindness ie. Respect and protect the female group, love and protect children and also help and protect the weaker sector of the society as a whole to keep the balance of Dharamic freedom.

Dharam cannot be called with any particular name, as no name exists as a concept of the reality while in fact the pronoun is the concept of reality. It is therefore, such systems make the Dharam limited and divide the society into units, which further causes serious problems in the society as a whole. The Dharam always condemn any form of split in the society, which is just the product of some irresponsible elements as to rule over others but their life always exists for a short period.

Dharam is the only ingenuity of expedient, through which any one can practice to understand that, ultimately there is only one Supreme, the creator of all living beings. Thus all the creations come from and the same return to Thy–Glory. Since the body of all the living beings, are appeared from the fundamental elements, through which the Aatma (Soul) transmigrates again and again for exercising to achieve the ultimate place, Heaven. At that stage the Aatma possesses no any form of body and thus the same becomes Permaatma.

The ones' who acquire a certain degree of Spiritual powers they represent the Supreme to control Thy creations accordingly, when and where they are required. The ones' who follow and adopt the principles of Dharam in life, they are the ones' who live forever but the ones' who later begin to misuse those powers, create an unpleasant and unstable society, in which the lives of all the people become unbearable. Then the Supreme Power presents Thyself into those living beings, the ones' who are just about to enter into Thy Perm Dham (Heaven) and then creates a balance of power between good and evil by counteracting and gradually diffusing the evil force that exists to maintain peace and happiness on the earth. Satya–Mev–Jayate.

The ones' who play such a role, are only considered as a messenger of the Supreme and the same, know nothing of the circumstances they are put in but as they achieve the goal over a particular situation then they are regarded with an appropriate title, i.e., Bhagwan, Prophet, Guru, Mahanaatma, Mahandev, Mahanbevi, Saint, Sant, Sadhu, Lord, Rishi or Muni etc.

Aartee

Aartee (Absolute Surrender to Thee–Divine) Divine) Divine)

- Aum Jay Jag Dish Ha–Ra, Swami Jai Jag Dish Ha–Ra,
- Bhagt–jano ka Sankat Kshan–Mai Door Kera–Aum Jay Jag ***Dish*** Ha–Ra...

Meaning:–Hail to Thee–Divine of the Universe, remover of sorrow of all Thy beings. I prostrate unto Thee–Divine.

- Jo Dhiyava Phal Pava, Dhuk Vi–Na Sawanka,
- Sukh Sam–Mati Man–Aave, Kashat Mita Tan–Ka–Aum Jay Jag ***Dish*** Ha–Ra...

Meaning:–The ones, who always remember Thy–Glory (The Functions) they are the ones, who live in their bodies comfortably and enjoys the glimpse of their life–circle.

- Mat–Pita Tum Mera, Sharn Gahun Mai Kiski,
- Tum Bin Aur Na Dooja, Aas Karu Mai Jiski–Aum Jay Jag ***Dish*** Ha–Ra...

Meaning:–Thee–Divine, you are the only refuge of all the functions through Mums & Dads thus how can I prostrate some one else?

- Tum Pooran Perm–Aatam, Tum Anter–Jami,
- Par–Brham Perm–Ieshver, Tum Sabh Ka Swami–Aum Jay Jag ***Dish*** Ha–Ra...

Meaning:–The Indwellers of all beings, Thou function is absolutely perfect, omnipresent, omnipotent and omniscient.

- Tum Karna Ka Sagar, Tum Palan Karta,
- Mai Savik Tum Swami, Kirpa Karo Bharta–Aum Jay Jag ***Dish*** Ha–Ra...

Meaning:–Thy Ocean of compassion, Thou function is the protection of all so keep on your benign services upon Thy Devotees.

- Tum–Ho Ak Agauchar, Sab Ka Pran Pati, Kis Vidi Milun Daya–Maya, Tum–Ko Mai Kum–Mati–Aum Jay Jag ***Dish*** Ha–Ra...

Meaning:–The life of all the lives, Thou function is the only one and that is still invisible, thus guiding me, the ignorant being towards Thee–Divine knowledge.

- Deena Bandhu Dukh Harta, Tum Rek–Shek Mera,
- Karuna Hath Bdhaao, Duwar Paraa Mai Tera–Aum Jay Jag ***Dish*** Ha–Ra...

Meaning:–Your function protect all the weaker in their strengths thus bless me with your compassionate hands I surrender unto Thy–Glory.

- Vishay Vikar Mitao, Pap Haro Deva,
- Shardha Bhagti Badhao, Santan Ki Seva–Aum Jay Jag ***Dish*** Ha–Ra...

Meaning:–Kindly relieve my all non existing suffering and bless me with ever increasing devotional trust in Thee–Devine love including the utmost spiritual service.

- Tan Man Dhan Sab–Kush Ha Tera, Swami Sab–Kush Ha Tera,
- Tera Tujh–Ko Arpan, Kya Lagay Mera–Aum Jay Jag ***Dish*** Ha–Ra...

Meaning:–My body including the feelings which are functioning along with the non existing forms are always yours thus without your blessing, nothing can belong to me.